Being Legally Blind

*Observations for Parents of
Visually Impaired Children*

Being Legally Blind

Observations for Parents of
Visually Impaired Children

Justin Oldham

Edited by
Griffith C. Steiner, MD

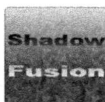

Shadow Fusion LLC
Anchorage

Published in the United States of America by Shadow Fusion LLC.

Library of Congress Control Number: 2010910977

ISBN 978-1-935964-00-1

If I could go back in time for just one moment,
this is the book I'd give my parents.

This book is dedicated to
every parent who has raised,
is raising, or will raise
a child who has a
visual impairment.

Your worries are not unfounded.
Your fears are not unreasonable.
You will do your son or daughter
a great service if your expectations
are fair, just, and attainable.

Contents

Foreword
by Griffith C. Steiner, MD

You hold in your hand a book of unique insight and value. As would be the case with most visually impaired people, Justin Oldham has a firsthand understanding of the many challenges this disability creates. Beyond his own personal experience and challenges, Justin brings tremendous sensitivity to understanding the trials and tribulations of his parents as well. Having previously published a spy novel and a science fiction short story collection, which are thoroughly entertaining and thought-provoking, he has proven himself to be a very experienced and talented writer.

Parents of children with visual impairments will find this book an invaluable resource. It will provide them with the ability to foresee the difficulties that both they and their children will likely encounter. Just as important, if not more so, is the inspirational message about how successful and fulfilling life can be for both children and parents facing this challenge.

His technical/medical understanding of his eye condition and the eye in general is remarkable. An ophthalmologist with additional fellowship training in cornea/external disease and glaucoma, I have been Justin's eye doctor since 1996. His detailed knowledge of the medical aspects of his eyes and their care is a credit to his intellect and curiosity. Although my profession revolves around the technical aspects of eye care, my undergraduate degree in sociology and my experience as a parent have led to my better understanding the deep importance of the parent/child relationship. That bond is even more important for a family with a visually impaired child. Justin beautifully demonstrates and shares his insight and deep respect for this relationship.

Justin brings notable intellect, curiosity, and empathy to all aspects of his life and work. This book is a wonderful example of these qualities and will be a great asset to all parents of visually impaired children.

Introduction

I am legally blind. I have what is called a congenital birth defect. My parents each had family histories of certain illnesses which made it much more likely that I would be born with my particular disability. It's not likely that I will ever be cured. The long-term prognosis is that I will eventually become completely blind. I have known about this probability since I was eight years old. Though medical science is advancing at such a rapid pace that many of my visual handicaps have been neutralized, it's not likely that the cure for my specific problem will be found in my lifetime. I understand this, and I accept it.

I was born with a condition called aniridia. To put it simply, my eyes didn't form properly and they lack irises. The iris is the colored part of your eye that surrounds the pupil. There are many other disorders that are common parts of this disability, including glaucoma, cataracts, and corneal, retinal, and optic nerve abnormalities.

Visual impairment is a fact of life for millions of people around the world. Being legally blind means that we are not fully sighted, nor are we entirely blind. This rather unusual circumstance makes it hard for our doctors, parents, teachers, and friends to relate to us and understand what we go through. As we get older, it's up to us to find the words to ask the questions that will tell us what we need to know about our disadvantages so that we can make the most of whatever eyesight we have.

Like anyone else who is born with a disability, legally blind children learn to live with their situation. We find our own ways to cope. We may not like it, but in the fullness of time we learn to embrace our condition and make it a part of us. One of the most difficult things we will ever do in our lives will be to relate the facts of our disabilities to others. In many cases, we make the assumption that adults already know what we're talking about. The details of our disabilities are just so commonplace to us that we assume that the adults around us must know more about them than we do. We have our feelings hurt when our teachers and friends don't understand our explanations. Sometimes people think we're lying when we talk about our blindness.

There are things that the adults around us can do to help those we regularly interact with to adjust. Our doctors can tell our parents what makes us partially sighted, as well as what they can do about it. Teachers can help our moms and dads understand our educational needs and how to address them. They can also help us to read, write, and study in the same classrooms as normally sighted students. The same people who teach us and help us with our medical problems can help our friends to understand us. The people who will eventually be our friends will ask us a lot of hard questions. The adults in our lives can help us to make sure we know the answers and better understand ourselves.

As a child, I wished for a self-help book in much the same way that many parents wish for an owner's manual for their kids. I learned to read early, and it frustrated me deeply that none of the libraries I went to had any books that would tell me how to be legally blind. I asked my mother about this shortly after my seventh birthday. She told me that I was destined to be a famous writer. She looked at me with total sincerity and said, "It'll be up to you to write that book."

I'm not a doctor, but I am legally blind. I also have just one eye. At the time of this writing, I am 45 years old and I still can't find any books that will tell parents or their children what it's like to be partially sighted. Although she died when I was twelve, my mother was right on two counts. I am an author, and this is my book about what it's like to grow up as a legally blind person. My hope is that the parents of legally blind children will find something useful in these pages. Your child has just as much potential as you think he/she does. His/her chances for a bright and successful future are better than you may know. Partially sighted is just one small part of what he/she is. It's not who he/she is.

Chapter 1
What Does It Mean To Be Visually Impaired?

Parents who don't wear glasses or contact lenses have a hard time relating to the vision problems that their legally blind sons and daughters will face later in life. If they are well-read, they may be able to intellectually grasp the nature of the challenge, but they won't fully comprehend the scope and scale of their child's disability until they've had some experience with it. That may sound scary, but there is one positive thing to remember. You and your child will be learning about his/her disability at the same time. That shared experience will bring you closer together. It will also allow you to be a more powerful advocate for him/her in the future.

Sharing the learning curve with your child will enhance his/her self-esteem and improve his/her ability to speak for himself/herself later in life. If you can embrace him/her for who and what he/she is, he/she will know that it's possible for others to accept him/her, too. He/she will come to understand that being visually impaired doesn't mean he/she is worthless or deserving of prejudice. As he/she reaches adulthood, you child will desire and strive for the same kinds of personal and professional respect that you do. He/she won't think of himself/herself as helpless. As a result, he/she won't let himself/herself be victimized.

The doctors who specialize in the study and treatment of human eyes generally agree that most visual disorders are inherited. A wide variety of undesired traits found in the

DNA of both parents can mingle to create vision defects in their children's eyesight. Most often, these defects are characterized by poorly shaped eyes or eyes that have missing parts. Defective eyes don't process light in the same way that normal eyes do. In their own way, they are like broken cameras.

Like so many things related to medicine, eye problems come with their own complicated, hard to pronounce terms and definitions. The three most common infirmities associated with the eye are hyperopia, myopia, and astigmatism. Each of these problems can be caused by any of a number of disorders. It's not unusual for several complications to be included in the package. To make sure that this book remains small and affordable, I'd like to suggest that you be prepared to spend a few hours with your doctor over the span of several visits to discuss the specific conditions faced by your child.

Hyperopia is commonly referred to as farsightedness. As you would expect, this generally means that anything close-up or nearby is harder to see than it would be at a distance. People with this condition usually see better when people and objects are far away. People like me are the exception to that rule. I am farsighted, or hyperopic, in large part because my eye has no lens. Hyperopia occurs when a person's eye is shorter than the focal length of the lens and cornea.

The term "farsighted" can be misleading. You can only see well at a distance if you have a lens that can "accommodate," or change shape. If you have no lens, lost the ability to accommodate due to the natural aging process, or have more hyperopia than the lens can accommodate through, then you can't see well at near or far distances. Ironically, even though I am farsighted due to the lack of a lens, I can see better up close because the magnification effect of holding objects close is greater than the deficit caused by my eye's lack of accommodation.

Myopia is more regularly referred to as nearsightedness. This means that people and objects are harder to see at a distance. People with this condition see better when the person or object being viewed is nearby. Myopia always allows better vision up close. Myopia occurs when the person's eye is longer than the focal length of the lens and cornea.

Astigmatism is when everything a person looks at is foggy, blurred, or fuzzy regardless of distance. This condition is part of my aniridia. My astigmatism is caused by the fact that my cornea isn't spherical. I wear glasses to sharpen things up and reduce the fuzz.

Newborns are initially examined by general practice doctors who look for physical defects of all kinds in their patients. If the doctor sees that a child's eye isn't shaped properly, he/she will ask for a qualified eye care specialist (called an ophthalmologist) to take a closer look. The ophthalmologist will use very precise, specialized tools. That's when and how he/she will determine if there are parts missing from your child's eyes. This is how my own parents got the news. Except for some brief discomfort from the use of a bright light during the testing, these highly detailed examinations are totally painless to the child. Early detection gives your doctor a better chance of treating your child's condition. More importantly, that early warning allows you a chance to get used to the fact of your child's disability. The sooner you come to grips with it, the better off you—and your child—will be.

As your child gets older, he/she will be tested for visual acuity. This is to determine what amount of usable vision your child has. The eye doctor will ask him/her to read the letters and numbers off a Snellen chart. If you've ever gone in for an eye exam, you've done this yourself. The chances are good that you'll be in the room with your son or daughter while the examination is taking place. Those of us who are legally blind can't read very much of what's on that chart.

Most eye charts have between sixteen and twenty lines of numbers and letters on them, ranged in size from large at the top to small at the bottom. I have never been able to read anything except the largest of those symbols.

The eye chart is one of the tools that your family ophthalmologist will use to determine your child's visual acuity, or what he/she can see at about what distance, at various times throughout life. Normally sighted people are said to have 20/20 vision. This means that they see objects of a standardized size clearly and without glasses or contact lenses at 20 feet. Twenty feet is the standard benchmark for all vision tests. It's very common for legally blind people to have visual acuity ratings of 20/800 or more. When I wear my glasses, I have a visual acuity of about 20/400. That means that, what I see from 20 feet away, a normally sighted person can see at 400 feet.

It may not be obvious to you at first, but it really is up to you to decide what and how your child learns about his/her limitations. Doctor visits will be what you make them. If you react with fear, it's likely that your child will assume that he/she should be afraid, too. All children learn to be confident or insecure based on how their parents deal with them and react to various situations around them. You'll have this influence over your child until he/she leaves home. Reacting positively to the professionals who can diagnose and treat him/her will take the mystery and trauma out of those early visits to the eye doctor. In turn, this will make it easier for your child to accept his/her disability as merely being a fact of his/her world and allow him/her to be more able to explore the things he/she can do.

Chapter 2
What's It Like To Be the Parent of a
Legally Blind Child?

Blindness, whether complete or "legal," is one of the more difficult forms of disability to live with, whether you are the parent or the child. The hardest part about being legally blind is that you're neither fish nor fowl. You're not quite sightless, which is how most people understand the definition of the word "blind," nor are you exactly sighted. This in-between status will make it harder for teachers, friends, and the people you work with to classify what your son or daughter is or isn't. Being the parent of a visually impaired child means you will need to understand approximately how much eyesight your child has. Your ability to talk about your son or daughter's visual capacity with other people can mean the difference between your community's acceptance or rejection for both of you.

Parents who understand the nuts and bolts of their child's condition may still have a hard time talking about it with others. I know that my own parents didn't like to talk to their friends and neighbors about my disability. The truth is that you will eventually face the same prejudices that your son or daughter will have to overcome. When your child is legally blind, you'll have to overcome the same obstacles as he/she will, plus a few others that are unique to your status as a parent.

The birth of a child has the potential to change any parent's worldview. The birth of a child who has a disability can rock a parent's world in some very unpleasant ways. People who have no medical problems may hold certain prejudices, whether consciously or unconsciously, about disabilities that they are forced to confront when a doctor tells them that their child has a birth defect. Some of these prejudices form naturally. Others are the product of things that we've learned. The very tall among us may not think well of the very short. Those with a lot of muscles may hold low opinions about those who aren't as physically powerful. Those who can see well without glasses or contact lenses may believe that they are better than those of us who are visually impaired.

It's not unusual for some parents to hold on to their prejudices, even after they know the truth of their child's condition. I've met more than a few moms and dads who continue to relish such prejudices, yet everybody is supposed to understand that their biases don't apply when they are speaking of their own children. We can't all be saints, but we don't have to be sinners, either. Only you can decide when, where, and how to give up your prejudices. For many, the arrival of their legally blind son or daughter is enough to put out those fickle flames of smug, self-indulgent superiority.

My parents were both born and raised in strict, deeply devoted, religious families. My mother was perky, popular, and fashionable. My father was a handsome track star on his way to a meteoric military career. Both were frugal, with few vices. A tenet of their faith at the time I was born was that birth defects were a punishment from God. The news that I had a significant visual disability—that I was "broken"—hit them hard.

Of my parents, my mother was quickest to change her mind. She accepted me for who and what I was almost immediately. That opinion never changed up to the day she died. My father was a tougher sell. The knowledge that I had a disability hurt him in ways that I wouldn't understand until I was 15 or 16 years old. As far as I know, he didn't give me his official seal of total, unconditional approval until I graduated from college.

Successful parenting means more than just providing transportation, food, shelter, and clothing for your children. It means loving them for who they are and what they can do, not just focusing on what they can't do. It also means being a good example—being somewhat like the kind of person that you want your children, disabled or not, to be when they strike out on their own. That's going to require that you do more than teach, protect, and advocate for your partially sighted progeny. To be truly successful, you'll need to put aside whatever prejudices you may have about what it means to be disabled.

My parents didn't know anyone else who had a child with a disability when I was born. There was nothing like this book for them to refer to or fall back on, so they made everything up as they went along. They were shocked to discover that some of their friends turned away from them. Their feelings were hurt when some of the people they went to church with had harsh words. They suffered quietly when members on both sides of the family made disparaging remarks.

Your child's blindness does not define who he/she is, any more than it says anything about who you are. It does not prevent him/her from being a successful adult. His/her lack of normal eyesight doesn't curse you with bad luck or damn you to a fiery Hell. However, the existence of his/her disability will prove beyond any doubt who your friends really are.

Intolerance can be an invisible stain on anyone's character. Friends, family, and associates who pass hostile judgment on you because of your child's disability—which you couldn't predict or prevent—have larger issues of their own. The most unlikely people can show the need to feel superior to others. I've seen this weakness demonstrated by some of the most outwardly humble, intelligent individuals.

Being the successful parent of a legally blind child means confronting those dark social forces so your child won't suffer from them any more than is preventable. The example you set will form the basis of your child's understanding of himself/herself and his/her unrealized potential. When my parents stood up to their detractors, they showed me how to best speak for myself later in life. When they accepted me without hesitation, reservations, or conditions, I learned to be tolerant, too. When they encouraged me to try, I was given the tools to succeed.

Chapter 3
What's It Like To Be a Legally Blind Child?

The definition of legal blindness varies. For certain benefits, the federal government says that the person classified as legally blind must have a visual acuity rating of 20/200 or worse in the better eye. In many states, the law says that individuals must have a visual acuity of 20/40 in at least one eye or they will be denied a driver's license. For the average visually impaired child, none of this matters until he/she is about ten years old.

From birth until they can walk, most legally blind children do what all infants and toddlers do best. They eat, sleep, and deprive their parents of sleep in the same way that fully sighted babies do. It takes between one and three years for the average sighted child to develop his/her full distance vision. As his/her visual field expands, he/she takes interest in people and things that are farther away. A legally blind child's "distance vision" isn't very distant at all. As a result, the initial explorations of a child with low visual acuity may occur much more slowly than those of a fully sighted counterpart would.

Medical records from my young childhood suggest my distance vision was less than two inches until I was perhaps two years old. According to my mother, I spent a lot of time with my eyes closed until I could walk. Over the years, I've seen this behavior exhibited by other partially sighted infants. There's not much to see, but everything to hear. When a person lacks one of his/her five senses, it's common for the others to become more sensitive. Partially sighted children may not be able to see very well, but they often develop excellent hearing.

It may surprise you to know that your partially sighted child could learn how to develop a "sound picture" of the room he/she is in. Even as an adult, I do this without thinking about it. This is something that completely blind people of all ages do every day. It becomes a reflex. In much the same way that you learned how to gauge visual distances, we learn how to interpret what we hear. Practice makes perfect.

Just as no two children are alike, you should know that no two cases of legal blindness are alike. The causes of impaired vision are many and varied. Partially sighted is exactly what it sounds like. Partial means "some," so partially sighted means "some sight." It'll take a lot of trial and error for you to learn the extent of your child's limited visual capability. Even with the help of a doctor, you may have to wait until your child can talk before you'll be able to really understand what he/she can or can't see.

Blind babies need love, too. Physical interaction with your visually impaired child may actually count for more than it might with a fully sighted child. Legally blind children have the same mental, physical, and emotional needs as their fully sighted counterparts. Parents of partially sighted children should keep this in mind when they feel the urge to step back in an effort to develop some emotional distance between themselves and their children. This reaction usually occurs because the parent perceives the child as being too delicate. My own parents struggled with this temptation. My mother was afraid that she'd break me. My father wasn't sure I could survive the rigors of being the accident-prone child that I was.

Poor eyesight, in and of itself, doesn't diminish curiosity. All babies, regardless of their health, are aware of the emotional state of their caregivers. Your child relies on your "vibe" to know what's good and what's bad. Even though he/she may not be able to see what you look like or read your facial expressions, he/she knows every sound you make. Like any other non-deaf baby, he/she will eventually figure out when you're talking to him/her.

As he/she finds his/her words, your child will also be finding his/her place in your world. Because you are initially his/her sole source of information for most things, he/she will tend to think of himself/herself as you think of him/her.

Without ever knowing it, my father sowed a huge field of doubt that plagued me for many years. By the time I was five, I had just enough words in my vocabulary to understand that he thought that the prognosis for my future wasn't good. In his mind, being legally blind meant bad things. When he talked about me in the presence of other people, his words and tone communicated that negativity.

My mother's message contrasted sharply with what I heard my father say. In her mind, there was no doubt about what I would eventually become. Her warnings scared me when she talked about the troubles I would face, but her optimism filtered through even when she talked about me to other people.

Until he/she has enough words to ask the questions that you dread, your child will take you at your word. If you say he/she is good, he/she will think of himself/herself positively. If he/she thinks well of himself/herself, it won't hurt either of you so much when he/she asks the hard questions about his/her blindness because he/she won't fear the answers.

It's been my experience that parents from any walk of life can inadvertently impress on their kids that what they are is more important than who they are. As the mom or dad of a partially sighted child, you're in a unique position to avoid this mistake. Many people with disabilities were raised to think of themselves as the embodiment of their disadvantage. When what a person is becomes the focus of how he/she perceives himself/herself, it's not likely that he/she will reach his/her full potential, personally or professionally. "I am blind," can become your child's justification—or excuse—for everything. This negative mental image has the potential to become a bigger handicap to his/her success than his/her lack of vision. In your role as parent, you have it in your power to decide what being legally blind means for your son or daughter.

Sometime after my eighth birthday, both of my parents knew that I was me, not my blindness. I can still recall the moment when I knew that my father was becoming comfortable with both who and what I was. He was talking with a friend of the family in a public place when he said, "He can't see very well, that's all." This may not seem like much to you, but it meant everything to me. That small attitude shift told me that it was okay to be legally blind.

Chapter 4
Assistive Technologies

By the time your child is old enough to start school, his/her visual limitations will have been diagnosed and he/she will be equipped with several things that will help him/her in his/her daily life. Most education professionals refer to these items as "assistive technologies." Don't let the awkwardness or complexity of the term throw you. All they're really talking about are the tools that your child might need to lessen the effects of his/her specific vision impairment.

Blindness is a term that describes more than one specific condition. No two children have the same degree of vision loss. One size does not fit all. This means that your child's condition will merit a unique mix of treatments and tools to help him/her become more self-sufficient. The tools he/she gets from teachers and other qualified professionals will depend on his/her individual needs and preferences.

Glasses and hand-held magnifiers may be some of the very first personal-use technologies to which your son or daughter will be exposed. There's a lot of good news here. The glasses that help your child see better can do more than help him/her read or avoid tripping over things because the lenses are designed to correct his/her specific problems. This very important visual aid can allow his/her eyes to do their job without so much strain. In turn, this will allow him/her to better use what vision he/she has and potentially keep it longer.

It's common for visually impaired boys and girls to squint in an effort to squeeze out a little more magnification or to screen out very bright light. Doing either of these things for long periods can put a lot of stress on your child's eyes, which can cause more problems the in the long run. The effect is not unlike sore muscles in your arms. After too much heavy lifting, they just won't work right, even if you want them to. It's unlikely that permanent damage will occur from making the eyes work hard, but it can result in headaches and ocular discomfort (called asthenopia). Proper glasses and/or magnification will reduce this stress and make viewing things more comfortable.

Modern eyeglasses can be made of many different strong, yet lightweight, materials. Today's lenses are often made from plastic, which can be treated with ultraviolet and antireflective coatings that filter out unwanted forms of light and reduce glare. The way the lens itself is made will determine how ambient, everyday light enters the eye. In some cases, changing the way light waves are perceived can make a lot of difference in the quality of your child's vision. He/she may use one type of glasses for seeing things at a distance. Others might be used for reading or doing things that need to be seen up close. It's not unusual for some legally blind individuals to have several different pairs of glasses for a variety of functions. In my adult life, I routinely use as many as four different lens configurations in separate frames to pursue my hobbies and do my job.

There are some types of lens used by visually impaired people that look strange or unusual. Some look like bubbles. Others resemble fried eggs. Some even look like they were cut from the bottoms of glass soda bottles. Even today, some people refer to glasses made with this last type of lens as "Coke bottles." In spite of their unusual shapes, the ways these lenses function can do a lot of good for the people using them.

Modern eye doctors have a lot of training and experience to deal with your child's low vision needs. In addition to providing the right optical prescription, they can direct you to the people who can make the glasses. Opticians are people trained in the science of optics. They are experts when it comes to glasses. Using the prescription provided by your family eye doctor, an optician can answer your questions and help your child get what he/she needs.

Optical shops carry a wide selection of frames that come in many different colors and styles. This is important to know because some frames are more durable than others. As a little boy, I was hard on my glasses. When somebody didn't break them out of spite, I often broke them just being myself, while running, playing...and falling down. As an adult, I'm still hard on my glasses. I drop them. I sit on them accidentally. I sometimes lose them, just as anyone else might.

Allowing your child to have some say in the color and style of his/her eyeglass frames can help him/her refine his/her self-image. It can also give you some clues about how he/she thinks of himself/herself. If he/she doesn't show any interest in what his/her frames look like, you might want to consider talking with him/her about how he/she thinks others might feel about them. As a child, I wanted very much to be like everyone else. That desire influenced my choices in glasses. I felt better about myself when I looked like the people around me.

In addition to eyeglasses, there's a good chance your child will also be equipped with a handheld magnifier of some sort. The most basic of these items is a traditional magnifying glass. These can come in many different shapes and sizes. Some are attached to a lanyard or cord that can be worn around the neck. As an adult, I still use magnifiers.

When high-end magnification alone isn't enough, some of these small, portable magnifiers are equipped with an on-board, battery-powered light. I used a lighted magnifier in grade school, high school, and college. Some are small enough to fit in your pocket. In many cases, school districts or nonprofit disability advocacy groups that receive state and federal grants provide these tools to visually impaired students for no charge. If one isn't available for your child, they are inexpensive enough that you can buy one directly from a company that makes them.

Specialized glasses and magnifiers aren't the only tools you'll be able to give your son or daughter. In addition to short-range optics, there's a class of long-range optical devices called monoculars that act like small, hand-held telescopes. Some are small enough to be worn around the neck, while others are too large to fit in your pocket. Contemporary devices can be focused manually or electronically. Some battery-powered models have low-light capability and other digital enhancements.

It's true that having all these visual aids hanging around your neck can be a little conspicuous. Even so, the benefits are worth it. When your child can see what the teacher is doing from his/her seat in the classroom without having to get up and move closer, he/she will tend to be more willing to participate in activities and ask questions. Because he/she isn't moving around the classroom to see, his/her classmates will be less distracted by his/her actions and more likely to accept his/her activities as normal. As an adult, I still use a monocular when it's called for. Between glasses, magnifier, and monoculars, I sometimes have as many as six items hanging around my neck at once.

The key to avoiding embarrassment while using these technological toys is to use them long enough, and publicly enough, for the novelty to wear off. Your child won't be able to prevent the people around him/her from being curious about the tools he/she is using. I still run into this problem when I meet with large groups for the first time. I've learned that the best course of action is to satisfy everyone's curiosity so that they can get bored with my gear and move on to being distracted by other things. In school, I usually took a few minutes each semester to pass my gadgets around in a spur-of-the-moment show and tell.

There are other options when portable magnification won't help your child read. Large-print books have been with us for more than a hundred years. It's not unusual for a school district to spend several thousand dollars on new large-print books every year. These are reproductions of the same textbooks that everyone else in your child's class will be using. Generally, the only difference is that these volumes are printed using large type. The only concession to making the book more manageable might be a lack of pictures.

Audio books for the blind were introduced in the mid-1950s. Originally, they were recorded as long play (LP) records. As technology changed and portability became more important, they were recorded on cassette tapes. Today's audio books generally come to the visually impaired as compact discs. Modern digital recording methods are quite good, allowing your child to use any number of digital replay devices, such as CD players or MP3 systems. Headphones allow your son or daughter to listen to narrated books in almost any environment without disturbing others.

Large-print and audio books are almost always paid for by agencies or nonprofit groups that receive state or federal grants. If you have questions, it may be a good idea to talk with your child's teachers or school administrators. They can direct you to the appropriate special education experts who can tell you what you need to know about obtaining these tools. There's no shame in accepting these "free" items. After all, your tax dollars are part of what pays for them to exist.

Some visually impaired students have special needs that go far beyond the use of portable vision enhancement devices and audio learning aids. In some cases, their vision is so poor that they need help from more sophisticated and powerful technologies. Closed-circuit camera systems and automated reading machines can do what other support mechanisms can't. The same types of nonprofit groups and agencies that provide large-print and audio books also provide these large, expensive items. This type of equipment may be hard to transport and difficult to store, but it's well worth having.

Closed-circuit camera systems that are used to allow the visually impaired to read are called CCTVs. Contemporary models consist of a digital video camera system hooked up to a viewscreen. This can be a standard television set or some other type of monitor that's appropriate for your child's needs. Books, papers, and magazines are placed on a flat surface within view of the camera. What the camera sees will show up on the monitor. The user can adjust the image in many different ways. The images can be changed to appear larger or smaller, display in color or crisp black-and-white, or appear as white text on a black background. These cameras can also reverse the image to accommodate dyslexic users.

As a little boy in grade school, I used a CCTV almost every day during the third through sixth grades. The systems I used were loaned to me by the school district. By using this technology to make the words on a printed page very large, I was able to read just as fast as anyone in my class. Using the CCTV along with large-print and audio books helped me keep up with the others. Thanks to this very powerful tool, I was able to progress with everyone else.

Any school-aged child can worry about falling behind in his/her studies. Legally blind kids can feel particularly frustrated when they know they're not keeping up with the rest of the class. At times, they become discouraged and want to give up. As the parent of a legally blind child, you'll need to be aware of this. Both sighted and blind children need to learn good study habits. Your child might have all the technological tools he/she needs, but he/she might not know how to apply himself/herself to the task of learning.

There are many degrees of blindness, from moderate to quite severe. A child who is severely blind might not be able to make out people, places, or things at all. As a small boy, I couldn't see anything that was more than ten inches away. For some visually impaired people, this level of vision lasts for their entire lives. When glasses, magnifiers, and CCTVs don't work for them, they may still be able to use reading machines, screen reading software, and Braille materials.

Reading machines tend to be large tabletop units, but they will become smaller and more portable as time and technology progress. A reading machine uses a sophisticated optical scanner and computer software to "see" what's on a printed page. A computer-generated voice reads to the user, in the same way you read to your child. Modern devices are capable of reading very small type, which can allow your son or daughter to find out what's printed on almost any page. By using headphones, the user can listen and learn at whatever volume he/she prefers without bothering anyone around him/her.

Computer screen reading software is also available. These types of programs allow a user to use a computer without having to see the screen. The computer verbally reads the words on the monitor to the user. People using screen reader software can perform many of the same computer tasks as a sighted person, including writing letters, manipulating spreadsheets, and surfing the internet.

All of these technologies can be used at the same time your child is learning how to read Braille. Braille is a coded system of raised dots, which can be typed or printed on a page just like regular print. Although my vision was just barely good enough to let me read with technical assistance, I still learned the basics of Braille. My understanding of this writing system helped me to better understand my letters and numbers when I first learned them. There was some concern that I might lose what little eyesight I had, so I was encouraged to learn basic Braille "just in case." Your child's situation may be different. The educational and medical professionals you and your child work with will be able to advise you on the likelihood your child will need this skill.

The items described in this chapter are some of the most basic and ordinary tools available to any blind person. As time passes, new technologies are being created and experimented with that will eventually roll back the darkness. As a parent, you can take some comfort in knowing that these tools exist. They're often easy to find and obtain. Once your child can use them without embarrassment, he/she will find many productive and creative ways to read, write, and learn.

Chapter 5
Orientation and Mobility Skills

From the moment your visually impaired child is born, you'll face issues pertaining to his/her mobility. Doctors, teachers, and special education providers exist to help you understand what your child can and can't do. Because no two children are the same in temperament or personality, it follows that no two disabilities have the same impact on a person's ability to move around or take care of himself/herself.

The things that catch your attention motivate you to act or react. This is particularly true for children, even those with visual impairments. A blind child may still react to what he/she hears, even if he/she isn't seeing anything that makes him/her curious. As a small boy, I couldn't see much, but the sounds I heard caught my interest. What was that? What does it mean? There was only one way to find out.

The urge to move is powerful, even for the blind. Without physical movement, it's almost impossible to be very independent. As a practical matter, self-sufficiency is something that most visually impaired people aspire to. We tend to think of our capability to move around without getting hurt as a form of freedom. As a child, I never liked having my movements restricted. Too many questions went unanswered because I didn't have the words to ask them. I was frustrated in ways that I couldn't express. Being allowed to explore helped me to answer some of those questions.

It's not unusual for infants who can't see, or who see poorly, to avoid moving too far away from what's known. As a baby, all I could see was a thick, gray fog. Anything beyond the tip of my nose didn't exist. Since I didn't see anything that was worth investigating within my limited mobilityrange, I had little reason to explore what was around me. As a toddler, my curiosity got the better of me, and I finally started moving toward sounds that interested me. My mother used to joke that any noise related to food would be enough to have me trying to find it.

As the parent of a legally blind child, you'll have access to orientation and mobility (O & M) teachers. In the United States, your local school district generally provides these trained professionals. As they answer your questions, they'll be working with you and your child to teach him/her how to move around without getting lost, avoid colliding with furniture or falling down steps, and other skills that will make it safer for him/her to be more independent.

Loosely speaking, orientation is the act of figuring out where you are. Mobility is what it sounds like—self-propelled movement in an area. It's the capability to go from one place to another. With training and practice, your child will be able to do these things safely. As he/she gets older, he/she will be able to find his/her way around familiar places without your supervision. Being good at orientation and mobility means your child can find his/her way around schools, libraries, and other public places without relying on someone else to take care of him/her. As he/she gets older, his/her training will expand to include developing skills with various tools that will allow him/her to be more self-sufficient.

It's true that there's a lot to learn, but it's all going to be absorbed over the span of many years. With both you and your child learning as you go, you get to take it all in at the same pace. As with so many other things associated with your child's condition, support and understanding make all the difference. Teaching your child to move, explore, and do certain daily living tasks, including household chores, means asking him/her to overcome many of the things that bother, worry, scare, or intimidate him/her.

Fear of the unknown is something that everyone struggles with. You may have seen some very scary things in your lifetime. It's quite possible that you've heard some things that have frightened you. In many cases, the blind are more afraid of movement and activity than they are of what they see or hear. Bumping into the sharp corner of a table, rolling off a bed, or falling down a flight of stairs are some of the more common mishaps that terrify visually impaired kids. "If I move, I could get hurt, so I won't move."

Problem solved? No. That's what O & M instructors are for. They can help your child get past his/her fears by teaching him/her spatial awareness and sensory alertness. In purely practical terms, this means learning how to build a map in your mind. It also means learning how to use what you can hear, smell, and touch to figure out where you are and how to get to where you're going and do what needs doing.

The technical term used by professionals in the O & M field is "proprioception." Loosely translated, it means that you process what your senses, both internal and external, tell you without thinking about it   I used to joke with my O & M teacher about "using the force." Proprioception is really just a technical term to describe the act of being observant. What are you hearing? Where does that sound come from? What do you smell? Where's it coming from? Can you feel what you're standing next to? What do you think it is? Is there a breeze? What's causing it? Which way is it coming from?

The act of being totally aware results in what teachers and technicians call "spatial orientation." That means knowing approximately where you are. Within just a few months of being able to walk, your son or daughter will memorize where certain things are in your home. He/she will use those objects as landmarks to help him/her explore. My parents were careful to avoid rearranging the furniture so that I could have a static and reliable environment.

There's an old saying that goes, "out of sight is out of mind." With your help, and some guidance from a specialized teacher, your child will learn about the differences between one object and another. Apples and oranges are both fruits, but they are not the same. One is a citrus fruit; the other is not. They feel, smell, and taste different. This training also helps your child to recognize the differences between one person and another. Different people move and sound different. The simple truth is that once he/she learns how to pay attention to all of his/her senses, your child will know a lot without ever having to slow down.

There's a lot of abstract information that sighted people get instantly by looking at a person, a place, or an object. Of these miscellaneous facts, size, distance, and direction are the hardest things to explain to a legally blind child. That's why parents and teachers often go out of their way to provide literal hands-on experiences to the blind. Something you see in a single second can, in some cases, be understood just as rapidly by a legally blind child if he/she has the opportunity for a quick touch.

As a child, my sense of touch was so well developed that my mother taught me how to pick out fruits and vegetables at the grocery store. Because I knew where all the squeaky floorboards were in the house, I was pretty good at sneaking around. My dad liked it when I buffed his boots because I could feel where the polish needed to go without looking at them. I never actually saw the shoelaces that I eventually learned how to tie. I did all of these things with confidence thanks to the support and good will of others.

Your child can be well equipped for immersion into the school environment once he/she has learned some of the more basic skills taught by members of the O & M profession. However, in spite of all that your child can learn through training, there is no substitute for experience. That's going to mean a lot of painful encounters. On my very first day of first grade, while my parents watched, I fell down the stairs in front of the school. Yes, I had been warned they were there. No, I didn't listen. After that, I was much more interested in the locations of all the stairs I might need to "find."

O & M teachers track your child's skill progress by monitoring the extent of his/her day-to-day activities. They're looking for what's called "independent movement." How much does your child move around? How much does he/she do for himself/herself without any help?

In some rare cases, despite all the available support and helpful devices, some kids can't shake their fears. Before you become too concerned, remember that some people are, by nature, extremely cautious. Your child's caution may have as much to do with his/her personality as his/her visual acuity.

In my O & M classes, I learned how to use a cane. I used one off and on through grade school, and it saved me from more than a few accidents. Even so, I freely admit that it was one tool I just didn't take to, in spite of making such extensive use of everything else that was provided to me.

The cane is a very practical device. It doesn't need batteries, and comes in a variety of styles. Some are foldable, which means they're easy to store when they're not needed.

Canes are possibly the oldest form of assistive technology for the visually impaired. A cane is meant to be used like a probe. The user "sweeps" the cane back and forth as he/she walks. Using a light touch, your son or daughter can brush the end, or "tip," over the ground ahead to detect obstacles or changes in the makeup of the ground.

The sweep of the cane can be narrowed in small spaces, or increased in wide-open areas. Curbs, stairs, and other rises or drop-offs are easily detected between one and three strides before they are reached, giving your child enough time to stop before tripping or falling. Vibrations from the surface friction of the sweep travel up the length of the cane. With practice, your child can use this vibration to "read" the ground ahead, determining whether it is dirt, concrete, grass, or gravel.

A cane user uses the information gathered from each sweep of the cane in conjunction with what he/she hears and feels. Gravel crunches when you walk on it. The cane tip clicks on stone or pavement. Blades of grass provide a slight resistance and a swish as the cane passes through them. With practice, it's even possible for a cane user to feel the wood grain on a plank floor.

As your child gets older, he/she will learn more complex orientation and mobility skills—more "tricks of the trade," as it were. The maturing child's expanded vocabulary is what makes this possible. Improved communications allow parents and teachers to answer hard questions while at the same time passing on more complicated knowledge. The net result is that your child will be able to live a fuller and happier life without fear of traveling, or taking care of his/her own basic needs when you're not around.

Chapter 6
Blindness and the Cruelty of Children

There is no parent with a heart who can stand by while others mock, ridicule, or physically attack his/her child for the sake of spite or sport. It's even harder for parents to hear about such harassment after the fact because they feel like they should've been there to do something. The terrible truth is that your partially sighted child is in for a lot of heckling and harassment from his/her peers.

Adults and children don't develop prejudices in the same way. For most adults, it's a rational process. Adults harbor prejudices for a variety of reasons, both tangible and intangible. The intangible reasons for adult prejudice are usually socially derived and anecdotal. The history we have with other people affects how we deal with them. As decades pass, we sometimes convince ourselves to make judgments about entire groups of people based on the experiences we've had with individuals

For the average child, whether or not he/she has a disability, prejudice is a completely emotional process. Children judge the people and things around them on the basis of how those people and things relate to them. People, places, and things that don't resemble what they already know or can relate to tend to be classified as untrustworthy, unsafe, or undesirable. People that your kids don't know can be scary. Unfamiliar places can make some feel like they are in danger. It's not unusual for some children, particularly the very young, to move away from objects they can't identify as "safe."

There is no single definitive fact that accounts for an individual child's spite. If you go to your local library, you'll find any number of published opinions on the subject. Children's prejudices can motivate them to say and do some pretty shocking things. Parents of the legally blind often live in fear of the hate speech and physical violence that their child is likely to encounter when he/she starts school. As hip and cool as my own parents were, they were definitely not prepared for the first time I came home with a bloody nose.

As a legally blind person, I can tell you from experience that there are several things that motivate "normal" kids to beat up those with disabilities. The first and foremost among these is that some kids are bullies. These aggressive personalities come in all shapes and sizes. No victim is too big. No insult, prank, or punch, is too small. These people pick on the blind and the sighted. The disabled just appear to be easy targets because they are different. It's not unusual for bullies to have disabilities of their own. Choosing someone who is obviously different to pick on allows the bully to direct attention away from his/her own differences.

Whether they are children or adults, a select few bullies are either verbal or physical cowards. Of the two, verbal cowards are more rare. Verbal cowards talk tough, but they can't respond effectively to snappy comebacks. In many cases, they can be tricked into saying something that embarrasses them in front of the people they are trying to intimidate. Many of these hot-tempered individuals are very smart. Verbal cowardice often develops from personal insecurity, which in turn may be rooted in low self-esteem. Verbal cowards use anger as a shield when they've been insulted or mocked in a way to which they can't respond.

The physical coward is only slightly more common. These tough talkers bluster to keep their victims preoccupied by what they are saying just long enough to take them by surprise with a physical attack. Their own deeply rooted insecurities motivate them to preemptively dominate their victims. Violence is their best tool, so they use it. The element of surprise allows them to strike the first blow, and they often make it hard enough that the victim can't fight back. These loud, bragging people are also usually smarter than they appear. Their perceived public images as punchers and kickers make them appear to be less intelligent than they really are. Underneath their bellicose exteriors beat the hearts of worried individuals who live in fear of the day when somebody, anybody, doesn't bow to them. More specifically, they fear being kicked or punched as hard as they hit other people.

Bullies are the terror of every child's grade school experience. While they do prey on people without disabilities, they often seem to particularly relish tormenting those whom they regard as unfit. A child's world is very physical. Speed, strength, and the inventory of body parts tend to be the criteria by which children judge others. Bullying behavior is emotionally based. Playground bullies are still children. They haven't been around long enough to develop their rational thinking processes and are just as emotional as any other child.

While you won't be able to keep your child from being socked in the face by a bully, you can play a vital role in determining how he/she reacts to it and what he/she learns from it. By the time he/she starts school, your child will have begun to understand that he/she is different in some way from the people he/she learns and plays with. As much as he/she may know about his/her own disability, he/she is still learning about everything else that's not connected to his/her eye problems. That includes other people and what makes them tick.

What we think and what we know are two separate and distinct categories of information. As children, we don't understand that such a difference is possible. Both are muddled together in a mix of emotions and reactions to what happens to and around us. What we know tends to govern how we feel. The things that we suspect can make us anxious, curious, or afraid. If we're comfortable with what we know, we tend to be happy. Fear comes when we don't understand what something is or why it's happening. Even if your child is a bully, he/she will still be taken by surprise when he/she encounters other bullies for the first time.

Knowing that bullies exist isn't enough. I went to kindergarten and first grade armed with that knowledge. It didn't change what happened to me. My parents, with their comments and reactions, gave me the knowledge I needed to deal with those encounters. I can still recall my mother's kind words and my father's patience as I sat on the end of the kitchen table having my cuts cleaned and bandaged.

My mother begged me not to fight, explaining time and time again the nuts and bolts of human prejudice and fear of the unknown. With her pacifism came a clear and unambiguous truth: there will always be bullies. My father was far more practical. "You'd better get used to the idea that some people will try to hurt you for no good reason. Look out for it. Stay away from it when you can. If they won't let you walk away, stand your ground. Never throw the first punch. If they start it, you should finish it."

Children value the support of their parents more than they will ever be capable of saying. The fact that you reassure your child and explain why some things are the way they are shows him/her that you care and that you may have the answers he/she so badly needs. What you say to him/her after he/she has had an encounter with a bully does more than help him/her calm down and salve his/her wounded pride. It allows him/her to modify his/her worldview in a positive way that will benefit him/her as he/she gets older. Like so many other things that you do for your child, consolation and enlightenment will contribute to his/her positive self-esteem. He/she won't be so afraid of things that haven't happened yet.

He/she will be less likely to think of himself/herself as a victim. He/she will know bullies for what they are, and avoid them when he/she can, with the understanding that such a response is normal, expected, and wise.

The classroom is a highly structured and supervised environment. While playgrounds are usually monitored, they're still places where almost anything can happen. Most visually impaired children don't initiate the majority of their schoolyard fights. Even so, they are vulnerable to anyone who plays a prank or attacks, because they can't see their adversaries coming. In some cases, they may not even see them leave the scene. This also makes it hard for them to know specifically who pushed, tripped, or punched them.

Playground battles are going to happen, no matter how often you tell your son or daughter not to fight. My mother was adamant about that point. I tried very hard to honor her wishes, but things just didn't always work out that way. You may have taught your child what morals and ethics are, but it's hard for him/her to live up to those standards and ideals when he/she is under attack and retreat simply isn't possible.

As a persecuted little boy, I wasn't sure about a lot of things. Should I fight back? Should I tell my teachers? Should I tell my parents? As a parent, you want the answers to these questions to be an unequivocal, "Yes."

As an adult, your first impulse is to resolve the conflict. Because you care, it matters that your kids tell you when they're being picked on. For those who struggle in this socially difficult situation, it's not that simple. Kids learn early on that telling their teachers or parents about the bullies, teasers, pranksters, and jokers will get them labeled as "tattletales," or worse, by their peers, making their integration into the group even more difficult.

Children with disabilities crave social acceptance just as much as anyone else. From a child's point of view, it's not a good thing to have a reputation as an informer. This is why your child may not tell you about his/her troubles at school.

The loudest, most aggressive kids in his/her class will spread gossip designed to harm anyone who breaks this unwritten rule. Nobody likes to be considered untrustworthy.

When you talk with your child about his/her encounters with bullies, it's important remember that being blind doesn't make him/her defenseless. These situations will be especially terrifying for your child because his/her antagonist will tend to hit him/her—hard.

Stop and think about that for a moment. When a bully attacks, he/she tends to unleash far more physical force than you do when you swat, smack, or spank. Imagine what it would be like to hear your attacker and feel his/her blows without being able to see him/her! This is the ultimate nightmare scenario for blind kids when they think of playground perils.

It's tempting for some teachers to keep visually impaired children out of harm's way by restricting them to the classroom while the rest of the class is outside or by segregating them from other children on the playground. It's even more tempting for some kids to wish for that kind of protection. It'll be up to you to decide whether or not your son or daughter needs that kind of sheltering. Even if your decision is based on philosophical points that your child doesn't yet understand, it's important that you let him/her know you are taking his/her fears and opinions into consideration. The battles he/she wins today will make him/her a better survivor tomorrow.

There is a natural impulse among many blind and visually impaired children to disengage from any distressing situation, including verbal or physical attacks. You shouldn't confuse this impulse with a desire on your child's part to do the right thing. He/she just wants to stop the hurting. Depending on what you tell him/her about how to deal with these situations, he/she may walk away, run away, or fight his/her way free.

When you hear from teachers and administrators about playground fights, take the time to get your child's side of the story. If you think he/she did the wrong thing, take some time to explain your reasoning. Discuss what you see as the better way to have handled the situation. Come down to your child's level and make your case in words he/she can understand. Your experience with conflict resolutions can be very helpful to your child, whether he/she is visually impaired or not, if you can make him/her understand your point of view.

Remember to temper your understanding with realism. While most fights that involve your child won't be ones he/she started, some may be. Your child is just that—a child. He/she has the same emotions as any other child. He/she will form his/her own biases. These emotions and biases will cause him/her to act and react in the same ways as any other child, even if those actions are undesirable. Don't tempt your child to make his/her disability into a crutch that allows him/her to blame others for every bad thing that happens to him/her or to avoid the consequences of his/her own actions.

As scary as bullies are, they aren't the only threat to your partially sighted child's well-being. There are other things that motivate some children to form biases against others. Those who aren't bullies may still discriminate on the basis of perceived or demonstrated disability. In grade school, I knew several children who just didn't have much to say. So far as I knew, they were "normal" in every way. The teachers may have known otherwise, but other kids in my class teased them endlessly for being "slow."

No matter which school I went to, there was always a kid on crutches and another in a wheelchair. From first grade on through high school, a semester never passed in which those people with such obvious disabilities weren't teased, pranked, or harassed because they had notable physical differences compared to everyone else. I was glad to know those persecuted people. I counted many of them as friends.

At any given time, I could count on the fingers of one hand all the chronic bullies who inflicted their hate on me. As time passed, the numbers of those who teased or pranked me at any one school because of my disability ran into the dozens. Times have changed, but one thing has remained the same. The small number of bullies out there will always remain a dark force with which to be reckoned. However, the numbers of "normal" kids who pick on those with disabilities are a much larger menace to your child's physical and emotional security.

It's not unusual for visually impaired students to wear glasses with large or thick lenses. I have worn such glasses since I was five years old. You can still pick me out of a crowd just by looking at my eyewear. The specialized glasses and other tools that your son or daughter may take to school will attract attention. These technical aids, combined with the fact of his/her disability, will combine to form another obstacle to your child's acceptance.

The urge to make fun of other people is hard to suppress in children. "Funny" is just what it sounds like when you're a kid, and whatever makes you laugh is funny, right? Humor, and our perception of what is hilarious, changes as we get older. You probably know somebody who never lost his/her juvenile sense of humor, but for the rest of us, the definition of funny changed when we started to understand the difference between fun and ridicule. Most adults understand that it's okay to be the butt of a joke every now and then. The average kid doesn't make that distinction until he/she reaches puberty, or sometimes even later. For the grade school set, if something is funny, it's funny all the time. There's no concept of mercy for the person who is the target of the so-called joke.

For the person who is the focus of the jest, there is a sense of embarrassment that doesn't go away until well after the teasing has stopped—if it ever does stop. This is true for any kid, whether or not he/she has a disability. Mockery and slander are hard enough to tolerate when you're still learning about the power that spoken words have. Unfortunately, verbal gags often lead to invasions of privacy, including the theft of personal items. The victim can justifiably think that things have gone too far. When he/she doesn't know what to do about the teasers or the pranksters, the real suffering starts.

Your willingness to communicate with your son or daughter isn't enough when it comes to the hurts inflicted by discrimination and gossip. To combat these terrors, you'll need to be more than your child's trusted advisor. You'll need to be the keeper of his/her secrets. He/she needs to know that you'll hear him/her out without rushing to judgment. He/she will really want to believe you're on his/her side. You'll prove yourself worthy of his/her trust if you can hear what he/she has to say without becoming overly emotional. It's okay if you can't tell him/her how to fix the problem. He/she won't hold it against you. He/she's not sure what to do, either.

In early grade school, I learned that most of the prejudice aimed at me was often the result of what the other kids had learned from their parents. Those adults really thought that blindness was worth ridiculing. It's quite possible that they never discussed the subject with their children, but I had the bumps and bruises to prove that their boys and girls had received the narrow-minded message. During my school years, I also encountered a total of six teachers who held similar opinions. I was able to work my way through their misguided logic thanks to the many conversations I had with my parents. Thankfully, such prejudicial people were in the minority.

When I ran into these kinds of issues, my dad used to tell me, "We don't actually know what we're doing here. We're just making it up as we go along." I'd have turned out to be a different person if I'd had nobody to act as my advisor or confessor. My father was the "go-to guy" for solutions to my problems, while my mother was the keeper of my secrets. They didn't always get it right, but I always knew they were on my side, and that they were trying. As I got older, I became increasingly aware of just how bad my eyesight really was. That parental combination of sympathy and wisdom gave me a starting point—something to build on.

By the time it looked like I might live long enough to attend middle school, I was able to make some of it up as I went along, too. As children approach puberty, they tend to put a different spin on their prejudices. The things they decide to hate or laugh at don't always remain constant, particularly their prejudices about disabilities. There are some infirmities that it's hard to joke about, especially when the would-be humorist can't quite wrap his/her understanding around just what some disabilities really are. In other cases, the nature of certain disabilities is a little too creepy for some who can actually imagine what it might be like to have that kind of limitation.

Blindness is easy to ridicule. By the time most kids reach sixth grade, they've played games with their eyes closed or worn a blindfold at least once. Because they don't live with such a limitation as an everyday facet of their lives, it's fun, not scary. Even so, they grasp the basic concept. More importantly, they quickly learn how to exploit it. Verbal put-downs become less frequent while physical attacks become more prevalent. Pushing and tripping become funny because the attacker's "normal" peers can watch while he/she remains unidentified by the blind victim. Some consider the theft of a blind person's personal possessions while in the presence of fully sighted observers to be the highest form of putdown.

While the unenlightened may consider such things to be the height of hilarity, it's important to remember that the narrow-minded people who indulge in those activities assume that there will be no consequences for their actions. Their behavior is, to some extent, motivated by a sense of superiority, which leads them to be overconfident. This kind of egotism can be found in both children and adults who have no respect for others. This is an exploitable character flaw, and it becomes easier to defend against when your son or daughter knows what it is and why it happens.

Those of us who are blind tend to pay very close attention to what other people say. We are immune to certain social forces, like fashion, because we can't see them. However, we can hear what others say about us. As inexperienced and impressionable children, we are particularly vulnerable to rumor and speculation.

I learned early in my academic career that I could rob my detractors of most of their power over me by simply stating the obvious at the beginning of the year. In grade school, this meant a trip to the front of the classroom to say, "I am legally blind. That means I don't see very well. I have special glasses to help me read and I don't like it when stupid people take them away from me. Does anyone have a question?"

Prejudice is made possible by a lack of knowledge. By supplying my classmates with information, I took away the mystery surrounding my blindness. Using a two-word label to describe my condition was a sneaky move on my part, because I knew that most kids under the age of 12 will avoid anything that sounds boring or unimportant. When I said that I didn't like it when stupid people took my glasses, I was using the power of suggestion. Nobody likes to think of himself/herself as stupid. If only stupid people take the blind kid's glasses, most people will avoid doing it. These tactics didn't stop of all the mayhem, nor did they prevent me from getting beat up or having my glasses stolen. However, they did make those things happen less frequently.

This creative use of social forces and word play didn't work for me after sixth grade. Even so, I couldn't have made them work for me as well as they did without countless hours of time and attention from my parents. As I learned from them, they learned about me. Together, we battled and defeated the demons of my childhood.

Chapter 7
Playground Challenges

Recess and other scheduled play times offer unique challenges to visually impaired children. For most kids, it's more than just a time to play. It's a chance to shine compared to others. Classroom domination depends largely on brainpower. When boys and girls go outside to play, or even if they're getting their exercise in a large indoor area, they get physical. Size, speed, and strength become more important than knowledge, memory, or logic. Under these conditions, anyone who doesn't measure up to the group's standards will be singled out for teasing and other forms of abuse.

Visually impaired children are at a particular disadvantage under these conditions because they don't navigate in the same way that sighted kids do. Running across the playground at full speed isn't just an expression of pent-up energy and free will for a blind child. It's an act of bravery and faith. Your child can't see many of the obstacles in his/her way—until he/she runs into them. Even so, he/she may sometimes choose to run with the others because it's fun and he/she wants so very much to fit in.

Following the crowd and doing what others do is a behavior common to all children. Some social experts liken it to a form of herd mentality. Followers do what the leader does, all the while hoping that the leader does the right thing. As a legally blind little boy, I routinely found myself paying close attention to what others did. I walked in their footsteps.

I imitated what I could see of their movements. I did what they did when it appeared to work. With some trial and error, I learned how to minimize the impact of my blindness. I also learned how to fit in.

Grade school kids generally don't pay close attention to precisely how their peers do things. However, they do take notice when one of their own doesn't do something they regard as "normal."

Playing is perhaps the one universally "normal" thing that all kids do, but visually impaired children do play just a little differently than their sighted peers. Some boys and girls learn how many steps there are between the monkey bars and the swings. Others figure out how to memorize the feel of the ground in different parts of the play area. It's not unusual for blind children to touch every solid object they pass. It's like a biological form of GPS. Instead of a "global positioning system," you might think of it as your child's "general positioning system." Knowing where he/she is on the map of his/her world that exists inside his/her head can help your child avoid the fear and disorientation that can result from being in wide-open spaces, where his/her sense of direction and location might become lost or confused.

These basic survival skills matter. At some point, no matter how large the playground is, there will be a fight. In some cases, the teasing and practical jokes will go too far and feelings will get hurt. Things will be said and fists will fly. It's not unusual for normally sighted children to start these fights because they won't let up on the target, but it's also possible for your visually impaired son or daughter to be the instigator. Your child is still a child. That doesn't change just because he/she has a visual impairment.

There were many times in my childhood when somebody pushed my buttons just one too many times. Someone wouldn't stop hitting. Someone wouldn't stop teasing. I am very much the product of my parents' genetic get-together. I have my mother's brain and my father's tongue. I am just as stubborn as they ever were. When my rage boiled over, I moved in, fully prepared to seek, engage, and defeat whoever my opponent was. There were also moments when I picked fights that I knew I could win. I wasn't what you'd call a good playground buddy. I'll admit to working off some of my pre-teen frustrations, but I was also trying to send a message to the bullies that I wasn't an easy target.

It's true that grade school playgrounds can be frightening for the legally blind, but they can also be sources of great fun and enlightenment. Open spaces and unscripted playtime can motivate even the most visually impaired child to explore the world around him/her. The discoveries that your child makes on his/her own will be some of the most meaningful self-empowering things he/she ever does. Knowing this may help you to feel better about entrusting the safety of your child to school staff and teachers.

As a little boy, I couldn't see the bottom of the slide from the top. Even so, the climb up the ladder and the plunge down the smooth metal slope was a thrilling adventure. The sensations of gravity and speed fired my imagination. If I could do this, what else might be possible?

As much as I craved the thrills associated with a fast-moving merry-go-round, the implications of the monkey bars scared me to the point of nightmares. When I started school, I couldn't see more than two or three feet. What did it really mean to be "up high?" I didn't know, and that thought gnawed on me well in to second grade. As it turned out, the average configuration of monkey bars was just six feet high. When I conquered my fears long enough to climb on that cool, metal framework, I was disappointed and ashamed of myself for having ever feared to meet this challenge.

Fear of the unknown can make any child hold back, whether or not he/she has a visual impairment. It can also make him/her want to do some things that'll just drive him/her wild until his/her curiosity is satisfied. Every child has some degree of the need to know.

Being Legally Blind

As a blind child, I got down on my hands and knees in the puddles after the rain because I wanted to know what was under all that water. I learned about different kinds of rocks, dirt, mud, and worms. I couldn't see much of what I found, but I learned about smells and textures in a way that most sighted kids might not pick up on. As an adult, I'm tempted to regard those small discoveries as trivial, but I do know better. Even today, I still process what I can't see in textural terms. Crunchy peanut butter is rough with small sharp edges. Certain cheeses are very soft, but they still have a grainy texture. Nickels, dimes, and quarters are separately identifiable because they each have different images, are different sizes, have different textures on their edges, are different weights, and sound different when you drop them on a hard surface.

Your child can still appreciate birds, trees, and sun, even though he/she can't see them. Most people don't realize that blind people "feel" the space they're in. Indoors feels different from outdoors, and different sized spaces feel different. While it's true that some visually impaired people develop a preference for being indoors because they feel safer, it's also true that fully sighted people can develop agoraphobia, which is a fear of open spaces.

If your child shows a decided preference for staying indoors, don't mistake it for a phobia. Playground activities often provide the first really scary physical experiences that a blind kid has. It's only natural that that he/she should want to be away from something he/she doesn't understand, particularly if something in that environment has hurt him/her. It's up to you to make him/her understand that getting hurt on the playground is not the same thing as being hurt by the playground.

Chapter 8
What Is Special Education and Why Do I Care?

Parents of the legally blind spend a lot of time worrying about the special needs of their children. What are those needs? How do I satisfy them? These, and other, burning questions will torment your imagination and keep you awake at night. The good news is that there are a lot of state and federal programs that exist to provide the services or information that you could need. The bad news is that there are so many of these programs that you might not know where to start.

Medicine and social services have changed in many ways since 1965, the year I was born. Once a doctor diagnoses your child, you'll be swamped with reading and have a lot of questions. My parents learned about my condition by speaking with a specialist shortly after I was born. From what I understand, this conversation took about five or ten minutes. The doctor had no books or pamphlets to give them. As it turned out, my mother couldn't find the term for my condition, aniridia, in any medical dictionary she was able to look at before the spring of 1973. By the time I was ten, I knew more about my disability than my parents did.

Today, many hospitals have social service coordinators on staff who can help you get started. The various social service agencies and the programs they administer have different names in different states.

In the 1960s, academicians and physicians around the country were wrestling with the question of how to provide state-sponsored services to the disabled. By 1978, many states had developed a network of qualified service providers who held university degrees in a wide variety of subjects necessary to understand and assist people with many different disabilities. Federal and state funds allowed the creation of dedicated agencies tasked with dispensing tutorial services and useful technologies that could help anyone with a disability succeed in school. The tools and expertise at your disposal are considerable.

The term "special education" is misleading. While the label is technically correct, it carries a stigma that rapidly becomes all too familiar to disabled children in grade school. As you will eventually learn, people with disabilities generally don't like to be called "special." Any extra label that separates us from the general population is undesirable. It's hard enough to be different. The only specialized labels we want are those associated with the love of our parents and our personal and professional successes.

Eye doctors and teachers who specialize in educating the physically and mentally disabled often work together. It's not unusual for the teacher who helps your child to be on a first-name basis with the doctor who takes care of his/her medical needs. Try to think of doctors and "special ed" teachers as advisors for you and tutors for your child. They help you to be a better parent while they help your son or daughter to be a better student. There is no shame in allowing your child to make use of their services or allowing yourself to take advantage of what these individuals can tell you.

Your child's special academic needs don't mean you're a bad parent. Being familiar with those needs isn't a sign of weakness. It means you're smart. You're showing your son or daughter that it's okay to be partially sighted and that there are ways to adapt and succeed.

All of us learn things early in life that stay with us until we die. When those of us who can't see understand how to use the tools that let us learn at the same pace and in the same environment as our sighted counterparts, our blindness fades to a minor inconvenience. We earn the respect of others and bring home better report cards. This eventually translates into self-sufficiency and professional success. That's something that any parent can be proud of.

You may be surprised to learn that your child's assistive needs may not amount to very much. Those who are totally blind can sometimes carry most of the specialized tools they need in just a few pockets. Partially sighted students can use most of the same tools as their sighted peers. Your child may need magnification devices that come in the form of durable glasses or monoculars, which easily fit into pockets or hang on sturdy lanyards, for close-up or distance viewing. Individuals who read and write with Braille routinely own equipment that is no larger than a three-ring binder. Kids who are comfortable with having and using these things won't be afraid to use them where others can see. It's harder to tease somebody about being different when he/she doesn't show any signs of fear or embarrassment.

As you learn about your child's social and educational needs, you'll also be learning about his/her medical needs. In many cases, the two go hand-in-hand. The treatments and drugs that make the most of the eyesight your child has will also make him/her a better student. When I was in grade school, I carried my medications around in several small glass bottles topped by tiny, syringe-style eyedroppers. Today's pills and eye drops come in damage-resistant plastic containers. As an adult, I still carry my everyday meds with me when I leave the house. I have them with me when I go to give a speech, sign books, or wander around the mall. These portable, less breakable containers make it possible for your child to take some responsibility for his/her own well-being at an early age.

That said, keep in mind that many school districts have strong restrictions on what medications a child can possess and use on his/her own while on school property. Some schools require that the school nurse or an adult in the office dispense medications, and then only based on written instructions from a parent or medical professional. If your child has prescriptions that he/she must take during school hours, check with the school administrators to find out the rules that apply.

The medicines that keep your child's eyesight stable will most likely change over time. It's important that you make it clear to your son or daughter that pills, ointments, and eye drops don't have to be scary. Using prescribed medicines does not make him/her weak, wicked, or bad. Children who learn to use their meds responsibly are less likely to be attracted to recreational drugs later in life. They respect the power of chemicals.

With your advice to guide him/her, your child will grow up to value good health. Early treatment of the conditions that impair his/her vision will increase his/her chances for better eyesight, as well as better overall health, in later years. Like any other aspect of his/her education, your input and participation will make all the difference.

Chapter 9
Preschool and the Fight for Truth

It's not easy for any adult to acclimate to the role of parent. People who have no disabilities of their own often feel rushed when it comes to visually impaired children's development. The desire to go slow and be tender becomes overpowering. Many parents give in to this desire, coddling their children far more than is either necessary or good for either of them. Parents who have disabilities of their own may be better equipped to understand what their children are going through and allow them to work through the process at their own speed. Either way, the years pass quickly and the battles are many.

It's only natural for you to want the best for your child. As you learn how to work with the doctors he/she needs for the treatment of his/her disability, you'll find that your child will start to show signs of being the family expert on the specifics of his/her condition. That's because you and your chosen doctors will be among the very first people to answer his/her questions and teach him/her the details of exactly what caused his/her visual impairment.

Parents who participate fully in these early doctor visits can play an important role in their child's future academic success. Just by being in the room during the exam, you will help put your child at ease. When you say that it's okay to ask questions, you'll find that your son or daughter will open up to the medical professionals. When he/she is willing to talk openly about what he/she can or can't see, the doctors will be able to do more for him/her.

Most parents aren't immediately aware of one of the more positive side effects of these medical investigations. Legally blind children are just as curious as their fully sighted counterparts. Their need to know is just as strong as yours is. Children figure out a lot of things on their own, no matter how much vision they do or don't possess. Kids who learn how to ask questions also learn how to process the answers. It's not unusual for a child to feel uneasy or insecure about asking questions in a classroom setting. If he/she is afraid of others laughing at him/her or telling him/her that he/she is stupid, he/she will stay quiet. This fear doesn't exist in your doctor's office because there is no "right" or "wrong" in the quest for information about a medical diagnosis.

By the time I was six, my father was quite comfortable with taking me to the eye doctor. It wasn't unusual for us to have lunch before or after a visit. As we ate cheeseburgers one hot summer day, he said something that surprised me. "You're pretty smart. I wish we'd sent you to preschool." When I asked him what preschool was, he shrugged. "Nothing important for a smart guy like you." While missing preschool wasn't the disadvantage it could have been, that wasn't entirely due to my own natural abilities. A lot of work went into making that lack of preschool education not matter.

My mother was concerned that my blindness would slow me down when the time came for me to go to kindergarten. During the late 1960s, when I was growing up, there was some debate over the value of early education. Federally funded programs like the one that would eventually become Head Start were still new and very controversial.

In an effort to encourage my academic performance, my mother started working with me at the age of two. Think of it as an early, abbreviated form of home schooling. We used flash cards that she had made herself, of both letters and numbers. Thanks to her tireless efforts, I learned how to read by the age of four and write my name by the time I was five. I don't mind saying that I hated those flash cards with a passion by the time I blew out the candles on birthday cake number six.

Working like a well-rehearsed tag team, my parents took turns running drills with me until I got the lesson for the day. I may have missed out on preschool, but the many late nights at the kitchen table more than made up for it. My mother later remembered my first day of kindergarten fondly. "It was a thrill to know that you didn't have to see the blackboard. After what your father and I put you through, kindergarten was just a refresher."

It's not unusual for parents of legally blind children to think they're doing their kids a favor by skipping the "trauma" of preschool. While the academic merits may be debatable, the social interaction that preschool provides is extremely valuable. For a variety of reasons, visually impaired people often lack social skills that their sighted counterparts take for granted. The chief cause of this is the sheltering that many parents do out of reflex.

It's not unusual for parents of disabled children to think they are helping their sons or daughters by keeping them away from uninformed people who might say or do things that might hurt them. All children need to have social time with their peer groups. By allowing your child to participate with others in the preschool environment, you not only enable him/her to gain and practice his/her social skills in a structured setting, you allow others the opportunity to learn and grow from their interaction with him/her.

My mother was a very popular person in her school days. She was one of those people who everyone knew and liked—the proverbial life of the party. As much as she advocated for me and believed in my potential, she was always afraid that I might get my feelings hurt by people who didn't understand my situation. In an attempt to protect me from possible pain, she would sometimes give in to that maternal urge that causes parents to shield their children from things they can't stop, fix, or otherwise make better. My dad was cut from a similar social cloth, with one notable difference. He always preferred to look his detractors right in the eye. He tended to not shelter me from anything.

This philosophical difference provoked more than one late-night argument between them. In the end, I think they didn't send me to preschool more because they hadn't gone. When your child reaches that age, you'll have to make the decision for yourself. Even if he/she doesn't learn very much in terms of numbers and letters, he/she will gain skill in getting along with his/her peers.

People who don't have disabilities that impair their ability to learn can't relate to what it's like to be a blind kid in school. Many of the methods teachers use in formal education environments have a visual basis. That's a challenge that all blind people have to overcome. We spend our entire lives coping with a visual society.

In all but a few American school districts, you'll find special education teachers who can help make sure your child absorbs as much of the academic material as he/she is able. Keep in mind that there is no way they can inspire socialization. Being around kids your own age matters. Even if you can't see, you'll still be learning how to get along with other people when you study and play in close quarters under a teacher's supervision.

Chapter 10
Grade School and the Fight for Justice

Parents of visually impaired children often worry about the obstacles their sons or daughters will face in the classroom. This fear is completely normal. It's not enough to know that there are many state and federal support programs available to help your child. It's quite all right to say, think, and feel, that you want more than a bureaucratic response. That little "something extra" you're looking for can be found and harnessed in several different ways.

To make your child's grade school experience both positive and successful, you'll need to know three things about yourself. First, are you ready to fight your way through a well-meaning school system that's going to classify your child as a special needs case? Next, will you be able to deal with teachers and school district officials who will try very hard to impress on you the need for lowered expectations? Finally, are you prepared for your child to be mad at you?

Grade school is a lot of things. Today, it's typically thought of as the period of kindergarten or first grade through fifth grade. As we get older, we often purge bad memories from our subconscious while clinging to the good memories, which we might tend to overembellish. By the time we're 30, we've forgotten what it was really like to go through day after day of fear and uncertainty. This is true for anyone. Time heals many of our wounds, and we romanticize the past because we'd rather forget some of the more humiliating moments.

From the time your child begins attending school, you'll be fighting battles for him/her that he/she won't always be aware of. There will be moments when you won't like the labels that others attach to him/her. You'll get boiling mad when the people who are supposed to be helping seem to be hurting. There will be terrible moments of heartfelt pain and anguish when your child doesn't understand what's going on in the classroom or behind the scenes, or why it's happening to him/her and not to anyone else. The worst of it will come when your child focuses the full force of his/her anger on YOU.

Knowing all this ahead of time can give you a head start as you strive to anticipate your child's wants, needs, and fears. The truth is that both of you will be making the same journey at the same time. His/her worries will become your worries at some point. In the long run, your problems will also be his/her problems. You'll have a lot in common. These shared experiences will bring you closer together and make it easier for you to remain objective when he/she lashes out at you because his/her many frustrations have overwhelmed his/her emotional capacity to deal with them.

My parents struggled with the decision to send me to public school. They were told that a specialized school for the blind was the best choice for "somebody like your son." This turn of phrase is something that, even today, you'll hear a lot from school district officials and disability advocates. The language and phraseology used by educational and vocational professionals will tend to put you off. They don't use those words to put you in your place. The language they use reflects the profession they're in. They use the lingo or slang of their fields, just like anyone else.

Parents who decide to raise their visually impaired children with minimal government assistance often do so for a short list of reasons. In their quest to raise a "normal" child, they might want to avoid placing their child in a specialized school for the blind because they don't like the philosophy embodied in the curriculum. Many parents are turned off by the idea of their child being associated with organizations or institutions that play up the child's blindness. The unspoken truth for many is that they don't like the way teachers and administrators at these schools teach the students to relate to their disability. They may want their child to grow beyond the labeling of what they can't do. Some parents just don't like the idea of someone outside their family being too involved in what they view as the private matter of how they raise their children.

The people who want to help your child can sometimes strike you as being cold, uncaring, or unprepared. You might sometimes even think of them as adversaries. The truth is that each will be dealing with you and your child's needs according to his/her organization's mandate and training. The professionals who staff specialized schools have a point of view that you might not agree with. Their job is to use every state and federal program at their disposal to assist and educate your child. That's their bias.

It's important to understand just how cautious and reserved specialized schools can be. It's not their job to cultivate risk-takers. The rules and regulations that govern these institutions are designed to create survivors. The teachers who instruct your son or daughter have to observe those rules, just as you have to follow the rules where you work. Knowing this can make all the difference as you struggle to cope with the things you don't like about your child's educational options.

Depending on your point of view, the "program approach" to your child's education might be either comforting or scary. My parents didn't like the way that teachers in specialized schools taught their pupils to cope with their blindness. Many of these educators emphasized the limitations of the individual rather than his/her potential. The notion that the student needs to learn how to function inside the boundaries of their blindness tends to be overemphasized.

While this can result in a rapid acceptance of one's own capabilities, it can also foster a sense of inferiority that often results in an overly cautious nature and what some call a "victim's mentality."

One of the unintended side effects associated with the learning that goes on in these specialized schools is that, as the students learn about the world around them, they are also sent many soft-coded messages about their place in it. Teachers in these institutions often place an exaggerated emphasis on the state and federal assistance programs to which their charges may be entitled.

You may have heard the term "entitlement mentality." It's generally used to refer to welfare recipients or others who choose to remain on state or federal support rather than actively seeking employment. Many people also use this derogatory stereotype to describe certain disabled individuals who rely on publicly funded assistance programs. The cold, hard fact of the matter is that most children who attend specialized schools for the blind and visually impaired are led to believe that they should always be enrolled in assistance programs that will "take care of them." This can result in a child becoming an adult who thinks he/she shouldn't have to work, whether or not he/she has the capability of doing so.

Teachers and administrators who really want to help your child may see a need to emphasize these programs to ensure that your son or daughter always knows they exist. In decades past, it was common for both parents and children to be unaware of their legal rights and the existence of taxpayer-funded help. There's a redundancy built into these schools and bureaucracies that's designed to make sure that nobody ever goes without the tools, medicine, and services they need. Some parents will find this emphasis comforting and reassuring. Others will see it as interference.

Public schools are responsible for educating everybody, regardless of ability or disability. While it's true that they aren't geared to handle the most extreme situations, their mandate is to teach everyone to the same degree in an environment of equality. The rules and regulations that govern public schools tend to create more open, less sheltered social and academic environments. Each student is expected to exhibit a greater degree of self-reliance. Teachers and administrators follow rules and procedures that make this possible. The net result of this is that your child will be forced to take some risks that he/she would never have to consider in a more conservative environment.

As a parent, you want to do the right thing for your child. That's why this choice is so important. The people, places, and things experienced in school will enlighten your child and help him/her to develop into the responsible adult you hope he/she will become. It'll be up to you. You have to weigh what you know about your child and his/her personality against your own beliefs and concerns. Do you think he/she is a risk-taker who needs to learn a greater degree of caution, or do you believe he/she will benefit more from an approach that teaches him/her to be more independent?

The justice you're hoping for won't happen without your input. The decision my parents made for me may not be the right one for you. It's not unusual for blind or visually impaired people to have other disabilities that complicate their lives. These added factors may make it necessary for your son or daughter to live within some very precise boundaries. There is no shame in opting for a more conservative approach if that's what you think your child will need to live a full and productive life on his/her own terms.

No matter which educational option you choose, you're always going to hear from people who disagree with you. You could be surprised at how much opposition you face if you decide to send your child to public school. Federal, state, and local officials of all sorts will be armed and ready with lots of good intentions and rational arguments designed to change your mind. There will be many painful moments during which you'll be convinced that you've made the wrong decision. These conflicts may not end until your son or daughter has graduated from high school, college, or vocational or technical school.

Chapter 11
The Politics of Peer Groups

From the moment your legally blind child leaves home to begin grade school, you'll be an outsider in his/her world. This may be the first time your relationship with your child is redefined. It certainly won't be the last. All families, whether or not they contain children who are disabled, undergo this transformation. It's part of any child's journey into adulthood. The good news is that you'll soon discover that you have more in common with your offspring that you may have thought possible.

Because I didn't go to specialized schools for the blind, I can't speak about those experiences. My parents decided that public school would be best for me, so that's what I'll address. In hindsight, I'm grateful I had the chance to take some risks. Thinking and acting beyond the scope of my physical limitations has increased my understanding of what I'm really capable of. I couldn't have written this book if I'd been any less challenged, motivated, or experienced.

Those of us who are born with limited vision don't react to the visual cues that spur the fully sighted to action. Even so, we have the same innate curiosity that motivates everyone else. When we go to school, we learn how to harness our emotions and instincts. Unfortunately, we can't satisfy our curiosity in the same ways as our sighted peers. Sometimes, we sit and listen. Other times, we move in close. We sometimes reach out with our hands to touch. Most of the time, we're misunderstood.

As an employed adult, you're probably used to office politics. Most of what you've learned about getting along with others in a coordinated group environment has come about through the process of trial and error. Your child will have similar experiences as he/she learns about classroom politics. His/her point of view will differ from yours, but you'll find that he/she uses many of the tactics you've long since learned.

You may be surprised to discover that your child shares many of your priorities and concerns when it comes to social and political skills. Being partially sighted or completely blind doesn't eliminate his/her need to fit in and understand what's going on around him/her. Because your child can't see what's on the board, projector screen, or monitor, he/she will process the things he/she is told in a different way. This also means he/she will deal with the kids around him/her in a way that won't be "normal" according to the sighted majority.

Though contemporary teaching professionals have received a lot of training that will help them better understand your child's needs and where he/she is coming from, nobody will ever understand your child as completely as you do. Even so, you can reduce your stress by talking with the teachers and administrators who run the school that your child will attend. Asking them to identify the tools that will be available to your son or daughter isn't wrong, pushy, or intrusive. It's an intelligent approach to allowing your child to get the most out of his/her education. The explanations these individuals provide will help you get your child ready for his/her scholastic experience.

In the United States, it's common for grade school children to learn in a single classroom from a single teacher. Getting to know your child's teacher may take time out of your day, but it'll be well worth the effort in the long run. When it comes to your son or daughter, you are the undisputed subject matter expert. You'll be able to tell the teacher things that will greatly improve his/her ability to help your child be academically and socially successful.

Today's partially sighted students can do more than learn on an equal footing with their sighted friends. As your child learns how to take criticism and fend off insults, he/she will discover how to be more socially capable and personally interactive. This means more than learning how to schmooze. It can mean learning how to be a good role model. As you may know from your own professional experiences, it pays to have others think well of you. It's not easy to be a good example, but it's worth doing because it means that fewer people can argue with you and win.

It could very well be the case that your child is the only disabled person in his/her class. It wouldn't be impossible to learn that he/she is the only one in the entire school. Whether he/she is alone or just one of many, he/she can still benefit from what you know about office politics. You can give him/her the knowledge he/she needs to get along with others. Answering questions and demonstrating an even temper while showing good manners can go a long way toward eliminating prejudice and persecution.

Knowing what some of the pitfalls your child may face can help you overcome them earlier, leaving you with more time to focus on the task of nurturing your child's curiosity and desire to learn. Most children have some resistance to academics at first. Yours may be no different. No matter who you are or how you do it, it's hard to learn how to read, write, and do math. Your child will have the added burden of learning these skills with tools and techniques that will seem strange to those around him/her.

Hand-held magnifiers, reading glasses, and electronics of all sorts will help your child use many of the same books and learning materials that everyone else does. Large-print or Braille books could round out his/her everyday kit. You should regard audio books and the player that goes with them as necessities, not luxuries. Any tool that helps your child stay in school is necessary. If these items are "normal" to you, it's quite likely that your son or daughter will think nothing of using them.

School districts across the country try hard to integrate disabled boys and girls into mainstream classes to show the unimpaired majority of students that it's not a bad thing to be different. As time passes, the long-term goal of every American school district is to change the way we all think about the things that make people different from each other, including disabilities. As we become more tolerant and understanding of each other and our limitations, we remove the burdens of fear and guilt from our children and the future generations of men and women who are born "different."

In spite of everything you know about your child's classroom challenges, there will still be a lot you're not going to know about. That's because your child won't tell you. This can be hard to accept if you've always been his/her confidant or confessor. There comes a moment for every parent when his/her child decides that it's no longer okay for mom or dad to be the keeper of his/her secrets. This usually happens by second grade. Think of it as the first step in a longer journey towards the development of your child's conscience and discretion.

Your kids will take everything you teach them and hold it up to what they hear from others for comparison. Blind or not, your child will match what you've told him/her against what he/she has learned at school. This may encourage him/her to ask you some hard questions. Being familiar with your child and his/her needs won't take away all the pain and embarrassment you might feel, but it will allow you to be a bit more honest. What you say is more important than how you say it. Your child won't care that you blushed or stuttered if you can make him/her understand and feel better.

My father used to tell me that the only stupid question was the one you didn't ask. My mother apologized repeatedly as she stumbled through her explanations. Their answers to my tough questions never seemed as polished as the ones I got from my teachers. Even so, I valued what my parents told me more than anything my teachers ever said. That's because I saved the really hard stuff for the people I trusted the most, and they always managed to come through in what I now know were emotionally difficult moments.

One of the drawbacks to public education is that, as hard as it is for you to explain your child's disability to him/her, it's even harder for the people who teach him/her to make those explanations. That's because public school teachers have to maintain some degree of objective distance from their students in order to be effective. They aren't the specialists you might find in a dedicated school for the blind or visually impaired. They can't answer all of the questions you or your child have because they don't know all the answers.

At some point, your child will ask his/her teachers some of the hard questions. In some cases, he/she will do this just to see if the teacher can confirm what you've already told him/her. I was guilty of this independent double-check on more than one occasion during my grade school years. It was hard for me to accept the gaps in my parent's knowledge, and I had a real burning need to know what they were hiding from me. Thanks to their patience, I eventually realized that there was no grand conspiracy.

Parents who fail to fully develop their child's understanding of his/her own condition can run into unexpected problems with teachers and school officials. It's not unusual for a teacher to be concerned when a visually impaired student in his/her class fails to adapt rapidly. The truth is that no public school teacher has the time to go one-on-one with any individual student for more than a few minutes each day. Legally blind children who seem to be confused or unwilling to perform assigned tasks are sometimes diagnosed as being in need of remedial help.

"Special education" and "remedial help" are two terms that carry enough weight to make any proactive parent of a disabled child cringe in fear and revulsion. That's because children who are deemed to need "extra" training or teaching time are more likely to be held back in grades or shunted off to segregated classes where they are asked to do very little in exchange for advancing to the next grade.

As the child of a career military officer, I had the privilege of living in many states in the continental United States. In every school district where I attended classes, there was an assumption made about my academic capability. Specifically, the administrators assumed that I surely didn't know how to read. I was, after all, legally blind. How could I be anything less than "behind in my studies?" The active role my parents had taken in my early educational development, combined with their efforts to enlighten me about my own condition, allowed me to shock and surprise my detractors more than once.

Your child's understanding of his/her visual disability is important. Preparing him/her for the perceptions of others and to understand his/her own strengths and weaknesses will empower him/her to be a more socially fit person. If your child thinks of himself/herself positively, he/she will tend to achieve more academically than he/she might if he/she labored under a cloud of uncertainty. He/she may not be an outstanding student or a leader, but he/she will survive and thrive at moments when your attention is focused on other things. When he/she does well without your supervision, you'll find that you do well when he/she is not around.

As a working adult, you're familiar with the problems associated with workplace politics. Do you go along to get along? Do you run flat out to do the best job you can? Do you care about getting promoted? These are just some of the questions a child struggles to form and answer in grade school. This is just one more thing you have in common with him/her. Your advantage is that you already know the questions. You may not have the answers, but you can share what you know about the problems themselves.

Children of all ages, with or without disabilities, are subject to the same sorts of peer pressure that you deal with every day. When you praise your child's academic performance and expect him/her to work harder to get better grades, you're actually challenging him/her to excel in a way that breaks the unspoken "go along to get along" rule that you cope with in your workplace. This conflict between what he/she sees you do and what you tell him/her may cause your child some worry because he/she won't always know how to talk about it. That means he/she won't always share his/her concerns with you.

You could have any number of your own reasons for "going with the flow." Your decision to not work harder than anyone else could be keeping you out of trouble with the boss. It could also mean that you don't get as much flak from your co-workers. You might really like being "one of the guys." As a parent, you should be prepared for your child to make the same decisions for many of the same reasons.

Visually impaired children can, and often do, get good grades. As a legally blind student in a public grade school, I was bad at math. I was expected to be bad at math, and I was. Because my skills met their expectations, very few students or teachers ever razzed me about it. When I excelled at reading and writing, I rocked the boat. The other kids made fun of me. My teacher gave me a hard time. "If you can read and write so well, why can't you do your numbers?" Being the best at something made my life harder in ways that I hadn't expected.

My parents taught me to live with the insults of my peers when it was clear that the problem was their jealousy of my superior academic performance. My mother said, "You can't fault them for being jealous. They wish they could read and write as well as you do." My father was a bit more pragmatic. "There's always going to be somebody out there who does something better than you do. Don't apologize for your talent. Be humble when you're ahead of the rest, and be gracious in defeat when the others leave you in their dust."

Being blind doesn't mean that your child should hold back or accept second-class standing. It should never be an excuse for his/her failures, nor should it ever be the reason for allowing others to put him/her down. Your child shouldn't be afraid to embrace the same kind of professional work ethic that propels you to try harder and do more. If he/she is scared, let him/her follow your example. Once he/she knows that you have the same troubles, he/she will be ready to hear about your solutions. This really does mean that your life experience can work for his/her benefit.

Though children don't get "promoted" in the same way that working professionals do, they can earn a certain degree of status in their classrooms. Their station in academic life is just as important to them as your authoritative standing might be to you in your place of business. Blindness doesn't mean that your child has to be at the bottom of the social order. As he/she masters his/her lessons, he/she can also learn how to excel in the social skills that will one day allow him/her to enter the workaday world as a good citizen without a victim's attitude.

Chapter 12
Middle School and Academic Performance

Every parent wants his/her son or daughter to do well in school. Children with disabilities face an uphill battle when they strive to match the academic performance of their non-disabled peers. Grade school teaches the fundamental basics of reading, writing, and math. Americans think of grade school (also called grammar school or elementary school) as kindergarten or first grade through fifth grade. Middle school is generally comprised of grades six through eight. As he/she begins his/her sixth grade year, your child will be called on to use what he/she has learned. He/she will be taught new subjects that will help him/her explore the world around him/her.

When I started sixth grade, my parents became particularly interested in my academic performance. For the first time in my life, report cards mattered. I got the speech about the importance of good grades. I also got my first real taste of competition. "Good enough" was no longer acceptable. They told me that the grade school norm of going along to get along no longer applied.

When it's your turn to have this discussion with your child, you'll have to make your own decisions. How much value will you place on good grades? Is it a good idea for your son or daughter to develop a taste for competition? What do you consider "good enough?" This will depend on what goals you and your child set for his/her future.

Middle school is possibly the first situation your child will encounter in which he/she is judged on the basis of what he/she does and how well he/she does it as compared to other members of the class. It'll be up to you to determine just how hard to ask him/her to try for high marks. If you do decide to urge your child to work hard and study, study, study, you'll still be in for some challenges.

Teachers and school administrators who are sensitive to your child's special needs may counsel you restrain your efforts at pushing your child to excel academically. They may tell you to avoid getting your hopes up. In some cases, the person who gives you that advice might be too blunt. Hearing the words may hurt your feelings.

Before you respond, think about what you've already learned about your child and his/her abilities. The educators who are considering your wants and needs also have to consider how best to handle the large, and often thankless, job of helping many disabled students each and every school year. In addition to their heartfelt desire to minimize your child's emotional distress, they're also trying to be honest with you about what they believe are realistic goals to set. Add to the mix their mandate to ensure that every child receives the same degree of education in an environment of equality, and you can see how difficult a balancing act they have to perform.

Again, there is a tendency within the teaching and social service professions to foster low expectations of the abilities of the disabled. This is one of the most stubborn and persistent barriers you'll ever face as the parent of a legally blind child. It's not that these people want your son or daughter to fail. They just want both you and your child to recognize his/her limitations. In some cases, this can have unintended consequences because the people who do the teaching can be so thoroughly insistent. Chief among these might be a fear of success, or a falsely inspired expectation that it is desirable to be a person who knows and does nothing.

There are any number of reasons why your child might not be a superior student or excel in a particular course. You need to understand those reasons and accept them for what they are. Don't assume that your child isn't doing well in a given subject just because he/she can't see well. Don't lose hope when he/she is unsuccessful in learning a specific group of facts or a particular skill. Don't be afraid to show interest in your child's schoolwork. Do encourage him/her and help him/her sharpen his/her skills when he/she shows you he/she has a real talent for something he/she is learning in school. However, don't smother him/her with too much of your time and energy, either. Do what's needed and let the rest take care of itself.

I was bad at math. I have always been bad at math. Both of my parents lavished countless hours on me in an effort to improve my skills with numbers. My mother made and used flash cards, which I came to hate, loathe, and despise, because we worked with them so much. My father used a large jar of loose change to good effect, but not even that visual aid could bring up my grades. I can still accurately make change in my head, but I can't do anything more complicated unless I have a piece of paper, something to write with, and a lot of time to get it wrong. My teachers accepted my mathematical shortcomings, but my parents didn't.

Everybody is good at something. One of the many jobs given to your child's teachers will be to find out what some of those gifts are. No two legally blind kids are identical, any more than any two children randomly selected in any group are the same.

Nobody was more surprised than my dad when I proved that I had a knack for reading and writing. I was the kid who seemed to know everything because I wasn't afraid to go to the library and look it up. School district reading and comprehension test results indicated that I was reading at college level by the time I started seventh grade. My father, who had always been an intensely physical man, couldn't relate to that. By comparison, my mother wasn't surprised. She claimed to have known I would be a famous writer by the time I was five years old. She accepted my academic dominance in these subjects as only a proud mommy could.

Most school districts in the U.S. have specialized evaluation programs that can help you understand your child's academic strengths and weaknesses. Special education teachers can fine-tune your child's academic program to help him/her overcome his/her difficulties. Legally blind children routinely make use of assistive technologies suggested to their parents by trained and certified specialists. The glasses, magnifying aids, and low-vision reading material I used at home and in class helped me keep up with my studies.

It's not unusual for visually impaired children to need extra time to complete some classroom assignments. In many cases, the amount of extra time needed is minimal. Skilled teachers know how to give your child the added time he/she needs while keeping the rest of the class on task. When large blocks of extra time are needed, your child may be asked to come in early, complete work during recess, or even stay after school until the assignment is done. When that flexibility isn't available, you may be asked to supervise him/her while he/she finishes the assigned task at home.

Homework is a fact of life for any student. You did it, and so will your child. It's important that you have a good attitude about doing schoolwork at home. Any child, with or without disabilities, will almost always be looking for an excuse to avoid homework. Your son or daughter will follow your example. If you treat homework as if it's important, he/she will be more willing to do it. If you think of it as inconvenient or unimportant and he/she picks up on that, he/she will try even harder to avoid it.

As a career officer in the U.S. Army, my father had his own version of homework. On many occasions, we both sat at the kitchen table after dinner. He wrote his reports while I struggled through my math. His example and encouragement kept me from complaining more than I did. His praise made me feel better about what I was doing. In my adolescent mind, I saw myself as being empowered, decisive, and responsible. Even though I never did very well with math, I never considered giving up. I learned to accept that I wasn't good with numbers, but I also learned how to be patient.

It's not unusual for teachers in both public and private schools to think they're doing your child a favor by holding back on homework or excusing him/her from in-class assignments. I can recall several situations in middle school when a teacher told me, "You don't have to do this." I'd heard the same thing in grade school, and it frustrated me. It's true that some things that teachers have their students do are "make work," designed merely to keep them busy so they don't misbehave. From the educator's point of view, it may very well be a good idea to skip the busywork when they know your son or daughter is trying to complete the more meaningful assignments.

Most children feel pressured to complete in-class assignments and homework. That pressure is their version of work-related stress. Before he/she can excel at his/her studies, your child must be able to complete his/her work on time and correctly, in the same way that you do. Mastery of a subject comes from repetition and familiarity. Competence, as reflected in the grades on your child's report card, means knowing their subjects inside and out. This is no different than the level of skill you are expected to demonstrate each day in your job.

You don't like homework any more than your son or daughter does. You also don't like being pushed to do things you're not good at doing. Keep this in mind as you guide and encourage your child through middle school. The fear of failure common among the visually impaired stems from their worries over what they'll miss because they can't see. Visual aids and support technologies can make it possible for your child to be educated in the mainstream environment, but nothing short of improved eyesight will take away that fear of missing something important.

Strong support and consistent goal setting can do a lot to lessen these fears. Blind students don't pick up on many of the nuances found in public school education because most of the material is presented in a very visual manner. This can affect your child's academic performance in ways that are too subtle for him/her to tell you about. As hard as today's teachers and specialized disability technicians try, they don't always ask the right questions at the right time to discover the source of the challenges your child faces in learning a particular piece of material.

This is a short-term problem. It will be resolved as time passes and these professionals become more familiar with your child's specific needs and point of view. It's important to remember that nobody knows your child as well as you. Your relationship with him/her can greatly affect his/her academic performance. Your intimate knowledge of his/her aptitudes and inabilities can make all the difference.

Both of my parents went out of their way to explain the importance of good grades and higher education. Each related to these ideals in his/her own way. When I understood that their respective educations enabled them do the things they most wanted to do, I got motivated. Blind and visually impaired people have just as many professional aspirations as anyone else. All children, legally blind or not, have similar desires and expectations of their own performance. If you can make your child understand that he/she needs to know certain things before he/she can grow up to be a responsible person like yourself, he/she will think of his/her education as a path to success.

I've wanted to be a writer since I was a little boy. The help and support I got from everyone around me made that dream come true. The words you're reading on this page are the best proof I can offer that good grades do matter, whatever level of vision you possess.

Chapter 13
Middle School and the Struggle To Fit In

Pre-teens have a lot on their minds that can affect their performance in the classroom. Middle school is a transitional period for most young people. Their self-esteem is beginning to emerge. They're starting to notice the many differences between themselves and other people. Anything that shakes their confidence will distract them from the task of learning. As they pass through puberty, their emotions will play a greater role in their decision-making. The social behaviors they learn in sixth through eighth grades will, to some extent, determine what kind of adults they eventually become.

American grade school children spend most of their time with just one teacher. During the middle school years, the typical student is introduced to increasingly complicated material taught by teachers with particular specializations. This often involves going from one classroom to another for an average of six or seven lesson periods each day, with a different teacher in each class. Instead of interacting with an average of 30 people each day, your child might now interact with more than 200 students and teachers every day.

This increased person-to-person contact will affect any child. Your child will change. He/she will be forced to mature. He/she will also begin to resolve many of the unanswered questions he/she has about himself/herself. These are the same challenges and rewards that you experienced when you were in school. Knowing he/she will face many of the same things you did can make all the difference when it's time to help your child through his/her troubles.

Visually impaired children tend to remember more of what they're told than what they've seen. They don't always remember what they see because they've learned not to rely on their eyes. Audible memory is a skill. Sounds replace pictures. Kids who are blind from birth can become quite good at this without any encouragement from adults. With your acceptance and encouragement, it's possible for your son or daughter to develop truly exceptional memory skills.

It's not unusual for you, as a fully sighted person, to see a hundred people that you recognize in one day. You may not be able to remember all of their names, but you'll know them when you see them. As a legally blind person, your child isn't always going to know what somebody looks like, but he/she will usually be able to remember what that person sounds like. I never actually saw most of the kids I went to grade school with well enough to recognize them on sight. I attended a middle school with roughly 400 other people, and I might've actually seen 30 of them who got close enough for me to get a good look at them with my limited eyesight.

It's not wrong for your child to use whatever vision he/she may have. It's not strange, weird, or abnormal for him/her to associate the cloudy, blurry, or fuzzy images he/she has of other people with the voices that go with them. What he/she does isn't that different from what you do when you have a telephone conversation.

Chances are good that you talk to a lot of people on the phone that you've never physically seen. That lack of visual information has never slowed you down, or stopped you from doing your job. Lack of visual information doesn't have to stop your child, either, though it can slow him/her down. He/she might have to rely on people and things other than himself/herself to understand a concept that is being taught. Teachers, parents, and other students sometimes misinterpret this as "resistance." Teachers may misdiagnose it as a learning disability. Parents can unfairly think their child is being lazy. Your child's peers might decide that it's proof that there's something "wrong" with him/her.

When your child is bombarded with these negative assessments from all sides, it's possible he/she will become depressed or anti-social. As the parent, you're in a unique position to lessen these threats to your child's academic future and emotional health. What you say and do carries more weight with your child than what he/she will see or hear from anyone else. If you can understand how he/she learns differently, you'll be able to tell him/her exactly why it's normal, acceptable, and okay. Hearing this from you makes it possible for him/her to explain it to other people. As he/she learn how to explain, he/she learns how to anticipate questions. As he/she gets used to enlightening others about his/her condition, he/she will learn how to ask questions about unrelated subjects.

Before you can fit in, you have to be accepted. To be accepted, you must answer questions. This is a simple truth that applies to every person in every social group or business. Who are you? Why are you different? In a middle school environment, sometimes these questions are phrased crudely and with more than just a little prejudice. Being around more people means having more questions to answer and more opinions to sway. This is true for all school-aged kids, with or without disabilities. Because blindness is so foreign to sighted children, they're going to have even more questions than they otherwise might.

Teachers, administrators, and special education professionals are trained to ask the right questions. Even so, they won't always come up with the right solutions for your child's needs. You shouldn't blame him/her for this. It's a failure of communication that can be fixed by teaming up with your pre-teen to make sure he/she can speak for himself/herself in such a way as to be fully understood by the people around him/her. When that's not possible, it's up to you to save the day. Parent-teacher conferences and the occasional phone call can keep you in the loop when it comes to the needs and happiness of your legally blind child.

My mother died of cancer as I completed grade school. My father continued to speak with my teachers and school administrators while I was in middle and high school. In spite of every factually correct thing I ever told my teachers, I later learned that it helped a lot for them to hear the same information from my dad. Without his experience, credibility, and adult perspective, I'm not sure that my middle school experience would've been as good as it was. He helped me to find the words to deal with my peers, and to explain myself to the many teachers and special education experts who helped me.

With glasses, magnifiers, large-print and audio books, I was able to function in a mainstream classroom environment. I learned how to ask questions that served my interests while I kept up with class assignments and homework. I wasn't the best student, but I wasn't the worst. On paper, I was average. As you get to know your child as an individual, one of the things you'll learn about people with disabilities is that terms like "average," "regular," "normal," or even "nondescript" are desirable labels, ones that we will gladly wear. We know we could get stuck with worse.

Long before popularity becomes possible, acceptance is necessary. At some time in your adult life, a social or professional group may have rejected you for reasons that you still don't know. Even if you do know why, it doesn't lessen the disappointment. The struggle to fit in can take up more of your child's time than you might think. He/she can become obsessed with it. He/she may fear it. With your help, he/she can succeed at it.

As your child learns more facts and figures and how those pieces relate to each other, he/she also learns more about the world around him/her and the people in it. Socialization rewards the legally blind in two ways.

First, it's good to fit in, but it's even better to know how you fit in and why. Those of us with visual impairments tend to be at the mercy of the fashion trends and physical beauty that we ignore because we can't see them. There's a developmental opportunity here that most parents don't know about. As an adult, you'd call it self-actualization. As a kid in middle school, I called it "knowing who and what I am." By the time I finished seventh grade, I could relate a lot of what I knew about science, history, and math to my own situation. Discovering the "why" of things helped me to better understand myself, which motivated me to learn more. While this motivation didn't improve my grades, it did make me a better person.

Second, education is empowering. People who grow up with disabilities are at risk of losing some of that power. Absorbing names, dates, facts, and figures that can all be independently verified by almost anyone allows your child to eliminate the biases of his/her teachers and peers in a way that can't be misunderstood as a personal attack or creative lying.

When a classmate says something about your child that's not true, it can hurt if he/she can't find the reasoning or the words to disprove the charge. That's because he/she fears what you'd call "public opinion." He/she won't know how to respond to whatever charge is made because he/she can't see past the intent of the person making it. By the time your child reaches eighth grade, the natures and types of these attacks may become quite spectacular and pernicious. Something that sounds silly or totally unfounded to you runs the risk of becoming true to him/her if he/she can't stand up to the criticism.

Most discussions in middle school downplay the knowledge of the specifics behind why something is a certain way. That's really too bad, because the "why" behind things matters much more than you'd think to a person who can't see. As much as we're willing to take some things on faith, we're willing to entertain a lot more possibilities when we know enough about a subject to begin discussing abstracts.

Middle school curriculum stresses the realities of what is at a time when the average pre-teen is becoming interested in what might be. This can spark both great thinking and great criticism. It's not uncommon for social groups to form in response to what students learn and what they fear. Voluntary participation can result in clubs that cater to hobbies and specialized subjects or the formation of cliques that have prejudicial entry requirements to justify biases or protect the group's members from painful experiences.

I wasn't a fantastic student, but I knew my subjects and I knew a lot about my own condition. In grade school, I'd been a leader because I stood up for myself in a purely physical way that others found intimidating. I lost my physical edge in middle school. I became an outsider because I chose to ignore most of the available social groups. Over time, I formed my own social group, which survived until I graduated from high school.

My experience is not unique, or even particularly unusual. It's common for legally blind people to retreat from social groups that they think will do them harm. Good grades simply aren't enough to put an end to their fears of social rejection. As a parent, you have it in your power to help your child strike the balance that is right for him/her. Learning how to achieve good grades and good relations in middle school will pave the way for a happy and successful high school experience.

Chapter 14
What Can a Legally Blind Person Really Do?

My parents spent many sleepless nights wondering what kind of person I would turn out to be. They worried about the quality of my adult life. They weren't sure I'd be able to succeed in a professional, competitive world. The simple truth is that most parents have the same worries. Whether or not our children have disabilities, we all want the best for them. We can be quite upset when their prospects for success in something don't look very good.

You may be surprised to learn that history is full of notable people who were blind from birth. Homer was a Greek poet who lived sometime between 800 and 1200 B.C. Historians generally believe that he was born blind. He is best known for his epic poems about the Trojan War. His work was so good that it's still being studied today. Although he wrote his accounts several hundred years after the actual conflict, they are still some of the best sources for information about that turbulent period. By all accounts, he lived a long, productive life with very little medical or technical help.

The blind and visually impaired have played other roles in history that aren't as well known or so completely documented. The Romans used blind servants as skilled eavesdroppers to listen in on other people's conversations. During the Dark Ages and medieval era, it was widely believed that royalty and certain sneaky diplomats employed blind people as couriers to deliver important messages.

Throughout history, some tutors or private teachers for the rich and famous were blind.

Starting off with a visual impairment doesn't mean a child will grow up to be a failure. Partially sighted people have been making their own way in the world for more than a thousand years. Some have made significant contributions to the arts, sciences, nations, or causes they believed in.

Helen Keller (June 27, 1880 - June 1, 1968) is possibly the most famous blind American. She lost her sight and hearing as the result of a fever when she was about a year and a half old. With help from a gifted teacher, Anne Sullivan, who lost and then later regained some of her own eyesight, Helen overcame her disabilities and went on to do great things. As an advocate for the sightless and visually impaired, she dedicated her professional life to pushing for many of the social and governmental reforms that now make it possible for your son or daughter to be accepted by contemporary society.

In the modern world, legally blind people grow up to be lawyers, university professors, judges, and even authors, like myself. Marathon runner Marla Runyon became the first legally blind athlete to compete in the Olympic Games in 2000. In 2008, David Paterson became the first legally blind governor of the state of New York. I have known corporate executives who were visually impaired. I've even met blind people who use power tools in their woodworking.

We find our limitations mostly within ourselves. We've all encountered people who didn't believe in us or in our abilities to be productive members of society. Some of us went to public schools, while others attended specialized schools for the blind. In every case, we succeeded because we understood that we didn't need our eyesight to be loved, educated, or ambitious.

Even with the progress that has been made, the blind and visually impaired still face a great deal of prejudice. It's hard to get a job, even when you're qualified for the position.

Blind adults can talk for hours on end about the many people who try to hold them back for their own good. You can't make the false assumptions of others go away, but you can love your child and raise him/her to be a thinker and doer who is happy and motivated. Your gift to the future can be a productive member of society who doesn't conform to negative stereotypes.

Advancements in technology and medicine occur every day. There are millions of people around the world who dedicate their lives to solving any number of medical problems, some of which may relate to your child. It's important to remember this, especially when the harsh initial diagnosis comes. The solutions you need to make your child's life better may not come soon enough for him/her to directly benefit, but you'll see enough progress in your lifetime, and his/hers, to give hope to others.

As much as science and technology can help, they can't be counted on to do it all. The efforts you make as a parent will have a more direct effect on your child's outlook on life and his/her future success as a working person. It's not going to be at all unusual for you to run across people who think your hopes and dreams for your child are unrealistic. Your child will have encounters like that for as long as he/she lives.

Those of us lucky enough to have parents involved in our lives had our lives shaped by them, whether they helped or hindered us. You play a greater role in our lives than you know. Long before we receive our first taste of prejudice or enter a classroom, we are what you make us. The technology and medicine that will one day help us can't teach us the things you already know. Advances in these fields can improve the quality of our daily lives and make certain things possible, but they can't make us comfortable with who and what we are the way you can.

My glasses don't understand me. My medicine doesn't care if I get out of bed in the morning. The monocular that I sometimes carry in my pocket doesn't want me to be successful. For as long as she lived, my mother wanted all things good for me. That was important to me, even when I was a child. My father doesn't always understand what I do or why it matters to me, but he knows that I will struggle through until I either achieve success or learn a lesson that will help me later in life. When the chips are down, he's there for me.

My blindness didn't write this book. I did. I'm not afraid to share these things with you because my parents showed me, in word and deed, that it was okay to be visually impaired. I also learned a lot from my teachers and disability counselors, and I've used every skill they taught me.

There is more support available for your legally blind child than there is for you. Most of the help that agencies and hospitals are designed to provide is geared for the visually impaired child, not the parent. In some respects, you have a thankless job. No matter how rough things get, know that your child appreciates all you do to make his/her world a better, safer place to be.

I can't go back in time to give my parents this book, but I can see to it that it exists for your benefit. The things you think and believe are yours to share with your child when the time comes. The choices you make, and the answers you give, will provide him/her with enough knowledge and inspiration to be aware of, and comfortable with, who he/she is and what he/she is good at doing. His/her successes will be your successes.

Together, you and your child will conquer the prejudices associated with visual impairment. As a parent, you'll know just by watching him/her grow and mature that you've given him/her the good advice and support he/she will need to be happy and productive.

Chapter 15
Support Groups and Resources

Parents of legally blind children can sometimes feel very much alone. The need to talk with somebody else who knows about the types of problems your child faces in the same way that you do can be very hard to satisfy. Fortunately, in this day and age, you have a number of options.

If you take the time to look, there are several organizations at the local, state, and national or international levels across the country that are designed to provide services and information for the blind or legally blind individual and his/her family.

There are a number of national and international organizations that provide support and assistance to blind and visually impaired people and their families. Examples of these include the National Federation of the Blind, National Association for Visually Handicapped, and Lighthouse International. Such organizations act as advocates for individuals who are blind or have low vision, as well as offering services such as camps, scholarships, training, job opportunities, and educational tools and resources. You can find information on these organizations on-line, in the phone book, or at your local library.

Each state has a government agency that provides services to people with disabilities. The specific name of this agency and where it is located in the governmental table of organization differs from state to state. Your state's agency should be able to provide training, educational support services, assistive technology services, and listings of state and local nonprofit organizations that serve people with visual disabilities. The state government listings in your local phone directory should have a contact number for this agency.

Many states are also home to nonprofit organizations that serve the blind and legally blind community. Services they offer may include providing O & M training, job skills training, technical assistance, contacts for sources of products designed for the blind and visually impaired, and peer group interaction opportunities, such as summer camps, for people who are blind or have low vision. Some are affiliated with national or international organizations. Others exist independently. The agency in your state that provides services for the disabled should be able to point you in the right direction.

At the local level, depending on the size of your community, there may be a local parent support group. These can be more of a challenge to find than state, national, or international level organizations. Your child's doctor or the state or national blind support organizations may have suggestions for how to locate other parents who are also facing, or have faced, the challenges of raising a legally blind child. If there is local center for the disabled or specifically for the blind and visually impaired in your community, it will be listed in your local phone directory.

As time goes on, more and more resources are becoming available on-line. Using your favorite search engine, you can find support groups on the internet. From the comfort of your own home, using your personal computer, you can chat or correspond with moms and dads around the world who share your concerns. Using search terms like "legally blind support groups" can help you find what you're looking for.

When seeking these support services on-line, you need to be aware of the differences between chat rooms, discussion boards, and news groups. Each type of group can provide you with useful information and as much privacy as you desire. In some rare cases, you might learn things that you would rather not know.

Chat rooms are live, on-line environments where you can go to talk with other parents about the problems faced by your child. The "live" nature of these electronic message exchanges can result in some very passionate and angry moments. The people having discussions in this environment may come from anywhere in the world. It's important to remember that people in other societies and cultures may not hold your values. That means they may think of their children's disabilities in terms that you can't relate to. Don't take it personally.

Discussion boards are sometimes called bulletin boards or message boards. You'll find that the topics they cover are broken down into many different categories. The board consists of messages left by people interested in a specific topic or topics being discussed. You may not get an immediate response to anything you post, but you'll be able to type your message without feeling rushed. You can take some time to think or get over your anger or disappointment before you respond.

News groups, or newsletters, are information sources that you can sign up to get as regular e-mail. Most are free. In some cases, you will have to pay a fee to receive the information. For the most part, news groups function like newspapers or other on-line news organizations of which you may have heard. Some give readers the option to write in to ask questions to which the authors might respond. That's how a lot of newsletters develop new material. The authors write articles about topics that will interest their subscribers.

Generally, the only support groups you'll find were started by parents who have gone through what you are now experiencing. A few commercial sites do exist, run by operators seeking to make a profit while providing a service. In many cases, these sites generate their income by selling ad space on their web pages. In other cases, they charge their users a fee that can be paid by credit card. Other sites, run by non-profit groups, ask for donations, which can also be made using a credit card. Don't be afraid to look for and use the free services that are out there.

The number of websites and news organizations that serve the legally blind community is growing, as is their popularity. As your visually impaired child becomes an adult, he/she will have a lot to say about this communication tool. Using these on-line options will do more than make you a better parent. Your child will regard these services positively, and may even contribute to them later in life. Who knows? Your offspring could someday develop a website or write a book that's even better than this one.

Glossary of Terms

Parents from all walks of life can feel like they have to learn a second language just to keep up with their child's medical condition. The following is a short list of words and their definitions that your son or daughter will come to know, and use easily, as he/she matures. Learning about these terms now can help you communicate with your child and those who teach him/her and provide him/her with medical services as he/she grows into adulthood.

Acute: A diagnostic term meaning a condition that has come on suddenly. It can also mean that the symptom will go away in a short period of time.

Accommodation: The ability of the lens of a person's eye to change its shape to focus light waves traveling from near or distant objects. It can also mean a change in equipment or a process to allow a disabled person to participate in an activity as fully as a non-disabled person.

Advocate: A person who speaks for or aids a person who can't speak for or help himself/herself.

Amblyopia: Diagnostic term for a condition in which an eye doesn't develop its visual potential as much as is possible during a child's early development due to being out of focus or pointed in the wrong direction; sometimes called "lazy eye." The period of early eye development generally ends when a child is between eight and twelve years of age. Early treatment of the condition maximizes the eye's potential.

Americans with Disabilities Act (ADA): A federal law passed in 1990 [Public Law (P.L.) 101-336, 104 Stat. 327] that prohibits employers from discriminating against people with disabilities. This law will be important to your child when he/she is old enough to join the workforce.

Anophthalmos: Diagnostic term of Greek origin that means "without eyes."

Assistive technology: Any piece of equipment that helps a visually impaired person to function in an environment geared for fully sighted people. This includes magnifying glasses, audio books, reading machines, canes, and the like.

Asthenopia: Diagnostic term for eye strain or eye fatigue. Many people experience asthenopia as the result of forcing their eyes to focus on objects that are difficult to see for a long period of time. Symptoms may include headache, blurred or doubled vision, red eyes, or pain in or around the eyes.

Astigmatism: Diagnostic term for a condition in which light from a single point fails to focus to one point because the curvature of the lens and/or cornea causes the light to focus in two or more places. Astigmatism causes a person to see a blurred image, regardless of the distance of an object.

Baseline: Diagnostic term for how well a person can see before he/she gets glasses or contacts, receives surgery, or uses assistive technologies.

Binocular vision: Vision using both eyes.

Braille: Raised dots or bumps on paper that make up a form of alphabet that the blind can use to read and write. A person reading Braille does so by feeling the dots with his/her fingertips. Braille is written using a small machine that can punch through paper to create the dots.

Cane: A navigational aid for a blind person. This is usually a long, lightweight stick with a handle that allows the user to probe for obstacles one or two paces ahead of him/her as he/she walks.

Cataract: A clouding of the lens in the eye that reduces vision, regardless of distance.

Cornea: The clear, dome-shaped, outer layer that covers the front of the eye.

Congenital: Diagnostic term for a condition that was present at birth.

Depth perception: A measurement of how well a person can distinguish distances and dimensions of objects.

Diopter: Diagnostic term for the unit of measure of the focusing power of a lens.

DVR: Acronym for the Division of Vocational Rehabilitation, a state agency that uses federal and state monies to provide goods and services to the disabled. Most states have this agency, or a similar one with a different name.

Farsighted: See *Hyperopia.*

Field of vision: The area a person can see of the world around him/her without turning his/her head. This is often referred to as peripheral vision.

Hyperopia: Diagnostic term for a condition in which a person has clearer vision when looking at objects at a distance than when observing close objects; also called farsightedness. Hyperopia is the opposite of myopia, and occurs when an eye is shorter than the focal length of the lens and cornea. It is possible for a hyperopic individual to see well at both near and far distances when very young and at neither distance well once reaching the age of 40 or if extremely hyperopic. If a person has no lens, the lens has lost the ability to accommodate due to the natural aging process, or there is more hyperopia than the lens can accommodate through, an individual won't see well at either near or far distances. See also *Myopia*.

Individuals with Disabilities Education Act (IDEA): A federal law [Public Law (P.L.) 94-142] passed in 1975 which requires public schools to provide a free and appropriate education to school-aged children ages three to twenty-one, regardless of disability.

Individuals with Disabilities Education Act (IDEA) amendment: Passed in 1991 as Public Law (P.L.) 102-119, this federal legislation provides funds for states to serve infants and toddlers (ages birth through two years) who have disabilities.

LASIK (laser-assisted in situ keratomileusis): Surgical procedure in which the shape of the cornea is changed in order to correct myopia, hyperopia, or astigmatism. See also *PRK (photorefractive keratectomy)* and *RK (radial keratotomy)*.

Lazy eye: See *Amblyopia.*

Least restrictive environment: An educational philosophy. The idea is to provide disabled children with access to a classroom environment where they can study alongside non-disabled kids with as few obstacles as possible.

Legally blind: The standard a person must meet to receive certain benefits or services provided by governmental entities and nonprofit organizations. For many purposes, a person who is legally blind has fewer than 20 degrees of peripheral vision, less than 20/200 visual acuity in his/her better eye after correction by glasses, contact lenses, or other visual aids, or both.

Lens: A clear, flexible, curved structure within the eye that helps focus light on the retina.

Light perception: The capacity to determine the difference between light, dark, and shadow.

Light projection: The capacity to tell which direction light is coming from.

Low vision: Describes a person who has some vision but meets the definition of legally blind.

Myopia: Diagnostic term for a condition in which a person has clearer vision when looking at objects close to him/her than when observing distant objects; also called nearsightedness. Myopia is the opposite of hyperopia, and results from the eye being longer than the focal distance of the lens and cornea. While hyperopes may never see well at far distances, myopes always see things at near distances well. See also *Hyperopia.*

Nearsighted: See *Myopia.*

Nystagmus: Diagnostic term for a condition in which a person's eye or eyes appear to jerk or wiggle.

OT: Acronym for occupational therapist, a person who teaches disabled people how to function in environments outside the home. OTs specialize in knowing what unique obstacles to success your child will face in the classroom and around the school. Also an abbreviation for occupational therapy, the activities designed to teach a disabled person the skills needed to function outside the home.

O & M: Acronym for orientation and mobility. O & M training is a course or set of courses that most visually impaired people go through to learn basic navigation skills that can help him/her avoid getting lost or hurt while performing basic activities necessary to daily life.

Ophthalmologist: A medical doctor who deals with diseases and conditions of the eye.

Optometrist: A person who examines the visual capacity of eyes and prescribes corrective lenses, including eyeglasses or contacts.

Optic nerve: A bundle of nerve fibers that carries visual signals from the retina to the brain.

Orientation and mobility (O & M) specialist: A certified trainer who teaches the visually impaired to travel safely in buildings and outdoors while performing certain tasks which are important in daily living.

PRK (photorefractive keratectomy): Surgical procedure in which the shape of the cornea is changed in order to correct myopia, hyperopia, or astigmatism. See also *LASIK (laser-assisted in situ keratomileusis)* and *RK (radial keratotomy)*.

Proprioception: The achievement of total spatial awareness and orientation in an area by subconsciously focusing on both internal and external sensations and conditions.

PT: Acronym for physical therapist, a person who specializes in diagnosing and, in some cases, treating problems associated with a person's physical capabilities. Also an abbreviation for physical therapy, a course of treatment designed to maximize the physical capabilities of a person with low levels of physical ability.

RK (radial keratotomy): Surgical procedure in which the shape of the cornea is changed in order to correct myopia, hyperopia, or astigmatism. See also *LASIK (laser-assisted in situ keratomileusis)* and *PRK (photorefractive keratectomy)*.

Refraction: The bending of light waves as they pass through a substance, such as water, glass, or plastic.

Retina: A membrane at the back of the eye that is sensitive to light and that converts light waves into signals sent to the brain by way of the optic nerve.

TVI: Acronym for teacher of the visually impaired. This term is most commonly used by teachers and administrators.

Appendix
Suggested Reading

Brennan, Mary. *Show Me How: A Manual for the Parents of Preschool Blind and Visually Impaired Children.* American Foundation for the Blind, 1983. 56 pages. ISBN 978-0891281139

Castellano, Carol & Kozman, Dawn. *The Bridge to Braille: Reading and School Success for the Young Blind Child.* National Organization of Parents of Blind Children, 1997. 191 pages. ISBN 978-1885218087

Cavitt, William F. *Developing Self Without Sight: The Psychology of a Blind Child.* Authorhouse, 2006. 228 pages. ISBN 978-1425932848

D'Andrea, Francis Mary. *Looking to Learn: Promoting Literacy for Students With Low Vision.* American Foundation for the Blind, 2000. 252 pages. ISBN 978-0891283461

Frame, Melissa J. (PhD). *Blind Spots: The Communicative Performance of Visual Impairment in Relationships and Social Interaction.* Charles C. Thomas Publishing, 2004. 197 pages. ISBN 978-0398074746

Hall, Candace C. *Shelley's Day: The Day of a Legally Blind Child.* Andrew Mountain Press, 1980. 24 pages. ISBN 978-0960384006

Harrison, Felicity & Crow, Mary. *Living and Learning With Blind Children: A Guide for Parents and Teachers of Visually Impaired Children.* University of Toronto Press, 1993. 266 pages. ISBN 978-0802077004

Hermann, Spring. *Seeing Lessons: The Story of Abigail Carter and America's First School for Blind People.* Henry Holt & Co., 1998. 208 pages. ISBN 978-0805057065

Holbrook, Cay M. *Children With Visual Impairments: A Parent's Guide.* Woodbine House, 1995. 395 pages. ISBN 978-0933149366

Holbrook, Cay & Koenig, Alan. *Experiencing Literacy: A Parents' Guide for Fostering Literacy Development of Children with Visual Impairments.* Towers Press/Overlook School for the Blind, 2005. 66 pages. ISBN 978-1930526037

Kastein, Shulamith & Spaulding, Isabella. *Raising the Young Blind Child: A Guide for Parents and Educators.* Human Sciences Press, 1986. 208 pages. ISBN 978-0898852882

Landau, Barbara & Gleitman, Lila R. *Language and Experience: Evidence from the Blind Child.* Harvard University Press, 1988. 256 pages. ISBN 978-0674510265

Lear, Roma. *Look At It This Way: Toys and Activities for Children with Visual Impairment.* Butterworth-Heinemen, 1998. 160 pages. ISBN 978-0750638951

Maloney, Patricia L. *Practical Guidance for Parents of the Visually Handicapped Preschooler.* Charles C. Thomas Publishing, 1981. 78 pages. ISBN 978-0398045838

McLinden, Mike & McCall, Stephen. *Learning Through Touch*. David Fulton Publishers, 2005. 224 pages. ISBN 978-1853468414

Milian, Madeline. *Diversity and Visual Impairment: The Influence of Race, Gender, Religion, and Ethnicity on the Individual*. American Foundation for the Blind Press, 2001. 459 pages. ISBN 978-0891283836

Niemann, Sandy & Jacob, Namita. *Helping Children Who Are Blind*. Illustrated by Heidi Broner. Hesperian Foundation, 2000. 192 pages. ISBN 978-0942364347

Pereira, Perez. *Social Interaction and Language Development in Blind Children*. Psychology Press, 1999. 197 pages. ISBN 978-0863777950

Pogrun, Rona L. *Early Focus: Working with Young Blind and Visually Impaired Children and Their Families*. American Foundation for the Blind, 1992. 160 pages. ISBN 978-0891282150

Power, Paul W. & Dell, Arthur E. *The Resilient Family: Living With Your Child's Illness or Disability*. Sorin Books, 2003. 192 pages. ISBN 978-1893732667

Royal National Institute for the Blind. *Play It My Way: Learning Through Play With Your Visually Impaired Child*. Stationary Office Books, 1995. 125 pages. ISBN 978-0117016767

Stratton, Josephine. *The Blind Child in the Regular Kindergarten*. Charles C. Thomas Publishing, Ltd. 1977. 88 pages. ISBN 978-0398036232

Sullivan, Tom. *Adventures in Darkness: Memoirs of an Eleven-Year-Old Blind Boy.* Nelson Books, 2007. 240 pages. ISBN 978-0785220817

Index

About the Author

Justin Oldham is a legally blind writer who lives in Anchorage, Alaska. He holds bachelor's degrees in political science and history from the University of Alaska. A long-time Alaskan resident and self-described "reformed bureaucrat," Justin's many interests include collecting rare books related to the Cold War and 20th century science fiction, reading, writing, playing strategy games, and working on his numerous home improvement projects. Justin's other works include the novel *The Fisk Conspiracy* and the short story collection *Tales from the Kodiak Starport*.

For more information about Justin and his projects, visit his website at *http://www.justin-oldham.com*.

www.ingramcontent.com/pod-product-compliance
Lightning Source LLC
Chambersburg PA
CBHW071606040426
42452CB00008B/1261